VIEW OF
SUSSEX

VIEW OF SUSSEX

Described and
photographed by
BEN DARBY

ROBERT HALE & COMPANY

First published in Great Britain 1975

ISBN 0 7091 4722 8

Robert Hale & Company
63 Old Brompton Road
London SW7 3JU

Typeset by Specialised Offset Services Limited,
Liverpool and printed in Great Britain by
Ebenezer Baylis & Son Ltd., Leicester

Frontispiece:
Seven Sisters cliffs.

FOR DOREEN

CONTENTS

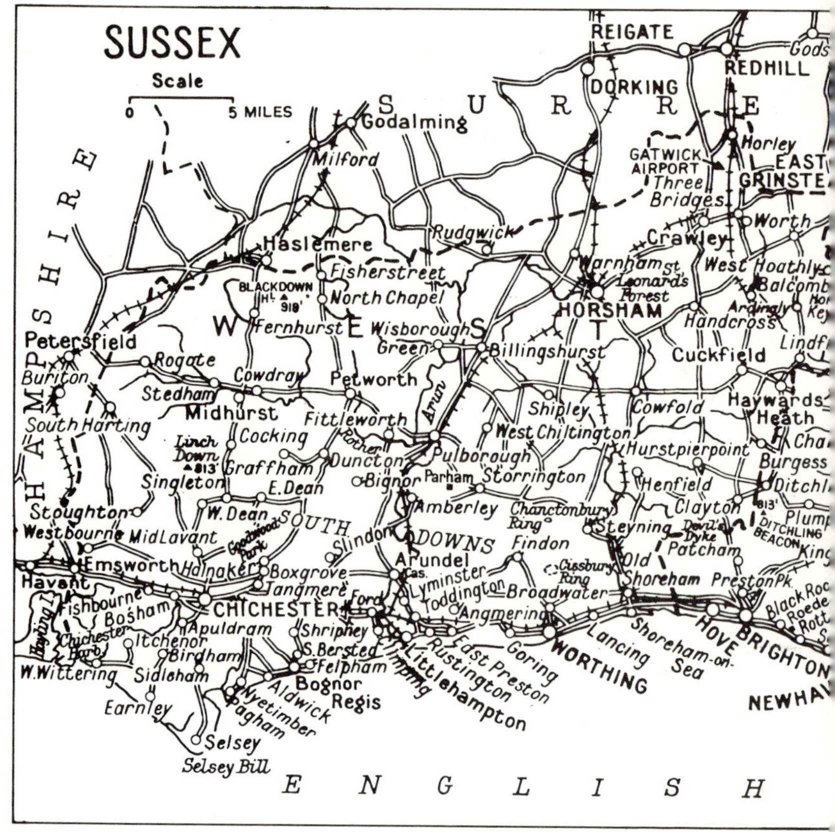

Map of Sussex.

Edenbridge
TONBRIDGE
K E N T
TUNBRIDGE WELLS
ASHFORD
Horsmonden
Groombridge
Hartfield
Lamberhurst
THE WEALD
Frant
Wadhurst
Tenterden
Crowborough
Ticehurst
Hawkhurst
Rotherfield
Romney Marsh
Nutley
Hurst Green
Isle of Oxney
Mayfield
Maresfield
Etchingham
Bodiam
New Romney
Buxted
Burwash
Four Oaks
Iden
Uckfield
Cross-in-Hand
Dudwell
Robertsbridge
Walland Marsh
Cade St.
Cripps Corner
Peasmarsh
Playden
Waldron
Heathfield
Rye
Lydd
Sedlescombe
Maynards Green
Dallington
Netherfield
Brede
Camber-on-Sea
E. Hoathly
Cowbeech
Battle
Rye Bay
Ringmer
E A S T
Battle 1066
Winchelsea
Dungeness
Herstmonceux
Catsfield
Upper Dicker
Ninfield
Windmill Hill
Glyndebourne
Glynde
Ore
Fairlight
Sidley
Hailsham
HASTINGS
Firle
ST. LEONARDS
Polegate
Wilmington
BEXHILL
Pevensey
Lullington
Long Man
Jevington
Westham
Bishopstone
Hampden Pk.
Willingdon
Friston
EASTBOURNE
Seven Sisters
E. Dean
Holywell
Birling Gap
Beachy Head
C H A N N E L

ILLUSTRATIONS

INTRODUCTION

In my teens and early twenties I rode all over Sussex, except for the downs, on a bicycle. The downs I explored on foot, walking the ancient ridgeway track many years before it became known as the South Downs Way. This is still the best way to see the Sussex Downs.

In the course of my travels I noted many variations in scenery and in vegetation, but could not wholly account for them. As a farmer's son, I knew a fair bit about soils, different kinds of plants to be found on different soils, and the varying types of agriculture likely to be practised on them. And nobody can live close to the earth and not realize that soil structures create the scenery. But I sensed that here was something unusual.

The downs were straightforward. The folds, the bold, sweeping lines and the fragrant sheep-cropped turf were entirely characteristic of chalk. Most of this turf has now been ploughed, and corn grows where the sheep grazed, but this arable farming is also typical of downland. The West Sussex coastal plain, with its brick earth and silt, bearing heavy corn and horticultural crops, could also be understood without much difficulty.

But the Weald was another matter. The Weald covers by far the greatest part of Sussex and its construction is complex. Cycling along the lanes of the forest ridge, which lies near the Surrey border, I often wondered how it happened that west of Horsham you passed abruptly from a light, sandy soil to heavy clay, and then, after a few miles, equally suddenly back to light soil, even sandier.

Then I found large stretches of a different kind of clay mingled with light loam and sand in East Sussex, a little south of Ashdown Forest. One thinks of clay as a sort of basic soil, the bottom of a pan, so to speak, but much of this clay in East Sussex is very evident at 600 ft. In the same area I found dramatic outcrops of sandstone rock, often in thick woodland. I loved the way the gold-green stone contrasted with the silver-grey beeches.

Later on, I found that geologists considered the Wealden area not merely unusual but possibly unique. Scientists still study it. A geological map shows that Sussex is made up of widely differing regions, and when you explore the county you find that these regions are sometimes separated sharply one from another, as, for instance, the downs are from the Weald, and that sometimes they overlap, as they often do in the Weald. The geological nature of each region dictates not only the kind of vegetation which grows in it but also, to a large extent, types of architecture and lay-outs of villages and towns. For example, you find buildings of flint on the downs but of sandstone on the forest ridge.

The history of Sussex is as interesting as its natural formation. You might say that history has trampled over Sussex. Stone Age people, Bronze Age people, Iron Age Celts, Romans, Saxons, Danes and Normans, all came this way, and all have left their mark. The Normans consolidated their Sussex bridgehead through a system not repeated anywhere else in the country. William split up the county into six strips, running south to north, and he put a trusted follower in charge of each. These strips were called rapes. A castle was built in each, defending a port, and each was named after the place where the castle stood: Chichester, Arundel, Bramber, Lewes, Pevensey and Hastings.

A wild and presumptious thought would sometimes cross my mind as I cycled and walked about the county. Perhaps, I thought, I might one day write a book about this unusual and beautiful countryside, but a 'different' sort of book in which a balance should be maintained between words and pictures, each complementing the other.

The thought remained steadfast with me through busy years of journalism, and now at last the opportunity has come to convert dream to fact. I dare to hope that this View of Sussex may contribute something to your enjoyment and even, possibly, to your understanding, of a county which contains every type of scenery to be found in Britain except mountains.

The parish church of Boxgrove village. There is nothing in this exterior view to prepare the visitor for the glory that waits within.

CHAPTER ONE

THE COASTAL PLAIN

If you stand on the 670-ft crest of Bow Hill and look south you will see spread out below a low and level land, and you will see nothing else like it in Sussex. The wide water and long inlets of Chichester Harbour thrust deep into the land, which is also patterned by the threads of innumerable streams and dykes. The sea shimmers beyond it. Over all the flat countryside soars the spire of Chichester Cathedral. This land is called the Sussex coastal plain.

The plain is roughly triangular with the apex at the eastern end and the base along the border with Hampshire. The downs constitute the upper side running south-east to Shoreham at the coast, which is the lower side. It is about thirty miles long and about ten miles at its widest. It is as flat as the Fens, almost as fertile, but less monotonous because there is always the backdrop of the downs, which on this, their southern side, are gentle slopes. The area embraces the city of Chichester, the little town of Selsey, and the resorts of Bognor Regis, Littlehampton and Worthing. Much of the coastline has suffered terribly from 'development'. Indeed, no open coast remains apart from Chichester Harbour, Pagham Harbour, a small stretch west of Selsey, and another small stretch between Littlehampton and Middleton-on-sea.

The whole plain is agricultural, and there is no open country, but it is a countryside of quiet charm once you are off the main roads. Lanes, paths and streams criss-cross it. You are as likely to see a thatched roof as a tiled one, and have as much chance of meeting a tractor as a car. It enjoys a mild climate which makes it suitable for outdoor produce which can grow nowhere else in Britain except south Devon, Cornwall and Pembrokeshire.

The plain has become one of the most important horticultural centres in Britain, with produce grown intensively both out of doors and under glass, and the value of this highly organized horticulture is reckoned in tens of millions of pounds. There were once fears that the big, new, wide-span glasshouses would mar the landscape, but, thanks to careful siting, they have not done so. In this small corner of England the first all-the-year-round chrysanthemums were cultivated. Commercial mushroom-growing also began here, and the growers of the plain, together with a few growers in other areas of West Sussex, still produce more mushrooms than any other county. Horticulture produces a great deal from comparatively little space, and most of the plain is taken up by arable farming in which wheat is the traditional crop. Very high yields are obtained every year unless the weather is disastrous. The corn men of the plain take the greatest pride in their crops and are disappointed if they are not the first in the country to start harvest.

Splendid elms were once the most distinctive feature of the plain. They grew beside the streams and the roadsides, in the hedgerows and along the headlands of the fields. They boldly broke the skyline whichever way you looked. In 1970 they were hit by an epidemic of Dutch elm disease, and in a horrifyingly short time thousands died, particularly round Chichester Harbour. It would not be true to say their loss has ruined the landscape, but, nevertheless, large areas, denuded of the tall trees, look strangely unfamiliar and forlorn to those who knew them before the disease did its damage. There will be other trees, but they will not be elms, and a tree takes a long time to grow.

Considering its size, Chichester Harbour is extraordinarily elusive. You do not see it from afar unless you are on the downs, and you reach its banks abruptly and in great

The saltings and mud flats of Chichester Harbour. Thousands of wildfowl winter here. The photograph was taken near West Wittering.

surprise. You then quickly discover that the word 'harbour' is more a comprehensive term for a district than for a place where ships tie up. The name itself can be confusing, for Chichester is two miles from the nearest wide water, though Chichester Channel pierces almost up to the city. But the name is of little consequence. The important thing is the place, which is beautiful, rich in wild life, particularly sea birds and waders, and is of vital historical and archaeological significance. It has also been designated an Area of Outstanding Natural Beauty by the Countryside Commission. It is about eight miles broad and five miles long and it is an enchanting world of open water, winding creeks, sand dunes, and extensive saltings and mud flats. It is bounded on the west by Hayling Island and the Hampshire coast, on the east by the West Sussex coast, and on the north by the A27 road. The fertile fields come down to the water's edge and you often find the nodding heads of the corn all but brushing the small waves that lap the banks of the creeks. High above the level fields and meadows, saltings and sand dunes, rises the slim spire of the cathedral, 277 ft high, the only cathedral spire in England visible from the sea.

The harbour is a highly popular yachting and boating area, and craft range from canoes to ocean-going cruisers. Even an area as big as this has limits and a careful watch will have to be kept to see that enthusiasm does not lead to overcrowding. In the meantime the continued zest for water recreation is supported by the establishment of sailing schools and boatbuilding yards along the harbour banks, and in the waterside villages the scent of flowers mingles with the scent of timber and tar. But the boat pictorially hauled half-way up the garden path is probably nothing to do with all this. It will most likely belong to the cottage at the top of the path, for the men and women who live on the harbour banks have been born to boats.

These are historic waters. Up the long reaches the oarsmen drove the Roman ships which bore supplies for the legions who took part in the great invasion of the first century A.D. Professor Barry Cunliffe suggests there was a port and supply base at Fishbourne, soon to become the site of a royal palace. It may well have been from this point that a young

This is the finest of the mosaic floors at the Fishbourne Roman palace. It is called the shell and dolphin floor and was laid about the middle of the second century.

commander of surpassing skill called Vespasian set out to conquer the west with the renowned Second Legion, subduing the Isle of Wight on the way. I often wonder whether Vespasian thought of the remote northern province, its wildness and its stubborn people, when later the cares and intrigues of emperorship pressed heavily upon him in Rome.

Professor Cunliffe's brilliant work on the Roman palace at Fishbourne has brought fame and fleets of motor coaches to this built-over area west of Chichester. Modern archaeologists are not only scientists but also artists, and under Professor Cunliffe's direction they have turned back the pages of time so that we can read with great accuracy the story of the magnificent palace which ranked with the great palaces of Rome. It was probably built about A.D. 75 for Cogidubnus, king of the Regnenses, whose capital was Noviomagus, our Chichester. King Cogidubnus was a man with strong Roman leanings, almost certainly familiar with Rome and probably educated there. The Romans thought highly of him. The Emperor Claudius appointed him Imperial Legate in Britain, which was as important as it sounds. He would have been an absolute godsend at a time when the Romans were gradually bringing Britain, with its squabbling though talented tribes, into the Empire as an entity.

In his book, *Roman Britain*, Dr. I. A. Richmond graphically brings home to us how highly the king was regarded by the Romans. In the eighteenth century an inscribed stone was dug up in Chichester. The words were a dedication to a temple and referred to the authority of *Tiberius Claudius Cogidubnus, rex et legatus Augusti in Britannia.* Dr

The geometric floors at the Fishbourne Roman palace are the earliest mosaics known in Britain. They were laid when the palace was built — thought to be about A.D. 75.

Richmond says this implies that Cogidubnus "had been endowed not only with Roman citizenship but with legatine authority within the province equivalent to that of a legionary legate, who had the insignia of a praetor, the second grade of senatorial magistrates. At the other side of the Roman world King Herod Agrippa had received comparable insignia, but not the legatine authority; and it is this conferment of Roman rank which attests in remarkable fashion the confidence felt in Cogidubnus by the Imperial Government."

Yet this powerful ruler is still to us a tantalizingly shadowy figure. Was he a just man, a man of intrigue, a cruel man, a kind man? Perhaps the picture will gradually be clarified as the archaeologists gradually clean away the film of time.

The regal glory of the palace at Fishbourne did not last long. There was a change of use about A.D. 100, perhaps on the death of Cogidubnus. The palace was split up into separate apartments, rather like flats. Part was demolished about A.D. 140 or 150. Disaster struck about A.D. 285, when fire destroyed the whole palace. It was never rebuilt. The walls were systematically dismantled and the material removed, probably to Noviomagus. Presently the Saxons and the darkness came and the wonderful palace of the king was entirely forgotten. A ploughman in the Middle Ages turned up some square, coloured stones. They meant nothing to him. Another workman in 1960 did the same thing with a mechanical excavator. He got off the excavator and reported it. The palace was found.

Though they may not be the most significant, the floors are the most striking feature of the palace remains. These mosaics, with their hallmark of high craftsmanship, reach cheerfully across to us over the centuries. The black and white geometric floors laid when the palace was first built are the earliest known in Britain. Later floors, in colour, were less geometric but more pictorial. The finest of these, laid in the middle of the second century, is called the shell and dolphin floor, because of its subjects, and it is practically intact. It includes a lively and now much-photographed sea horse.

The Romans may have established another port at Bosham. This is the most historic and one of the most beautiful of all the villages round the harbour. It is pronounced Boz-ham, not Bosh-am, and it is deservedly called the capital of Chichester Harbour. The little church is said to stand on the site of a Roman basilica built about A.D. 350. Roman stones and tiles are certainly incorporated in this church which is largely Saxon and could have been associated with a small monastery founded by a monk called Dicul with a small band of followers. Dicul set to work to convert the Saxons with depressing results. The Venerable Bede comments ruefully that "none of the natives cared either to follow their course of life, or to hear their preaching."

We should remember that the missionaries and monks who taught the Saxons were not so much trying to convert Britain as to re-convert it. In her book, *Weald of Kent and Sussex*, Sheila Kaye-Smith points out, "Before the end of the Roman occupation England was at least in part a Christian country, and the Saxon invaders overthrew not the altars of the Druids but the altars of Christ . . . it is a fact that much of Britain was Christian when the barbarians came. The invaders stamped it out entirely."

And much else besides. All the grace, art and civilization that was centred on the Roman British cities, including Noviomagus, disappeared. A brutish existence took its place. How much was lost we do not know. Only the patient work of the archaeologist can restore, little by little, some knowledge of the richness swept away.

The early Saxons of the coastal plain were, it seems, to put it kindly, more backward than most. This is not surprising. Forest and swamp cut them off on three sides and the sea lay on the other. They became very insular, and therefore suspicious of strangers. Isolated communities elsewhere in the county were little, if any, better. We do not know how able the missionaries were who came to the South Saxons, but they were certainly intrepid men.

Kent, immediate neighbour of Sussex, became the first English Christian kingdom. Sussex was the last. Conversion came from an unexpected source, and not after an all but impossible journey through the wilderness but from the sea. Wilfrid, exiled Bishop of Northumbria, came south. Once before he had attempted to land on the Sussex coast when driven towards it by a storm, but the natives drove him off. This time, in 681, they had neither the heart nor the strength to drive off anybody. Wilfrid, putting in to Selsey (Seal's Island), found them sorely striken by a drought of several years' standing, the consequence of which was famine. Wilfrid instantly decided to care for the body as well as the soul, and taught the inhabitants to fish. The Saxons had landed at Selsey in 477 but had not yet taught themselves to make fishing nets. Wilfrid stayed only five years but in that

The waterside at Bosham attracts sailing enthusiasts of all ages.

time he established a core of Christianity which endured and gradually spread through the county. He built a monastery, the church of which became a cathedral in 686, after his departure. The See of Selsey maintained an unbroken line until it was transferred to Chichester in 1075.

No trace remains of the cathedral, the monastery or the Saxon settlement. The sea has claimed it all. Erosion through the centuries has been steady and extensive, usually at the rate of about six feet a year. The local legend of a cathedral under the sea is probably true, but hopes of finding anything intact are small. The south-west gales will have seen to that.

Canute the Dane also had associations with Bosham and it is possible that his small daughter is buried in the church. It is therefore only natural that local enterprise should claim it was at Bosham that Canute gave his famous command to the waves. Alas, a number of other coastal centres make the same claim. Earl Godwin certainly lived at Bosham, and it was from Bosham that Harold set out on his unfortunate expedition of 1064, leading to his meeting with Norman William, the outcome of which gave William the pretext for invasion two years later. A good slice of the waterfront called the Quay Meadow is owned by the National Trust. Bosham, Itchenor, Birdham and Dell Quay are four of the best-known yachting centres on the harbour, and on a sunny day with a light wind blowing they present a picture you do not quickly forget – the blue sky, the flashing water, the white sails and the level land extending away to the rise of the downs.

South of Itchenor the harbour widens to meet the channel, and here are the Witterings, West and East, and here on the beaches in summer you meet the usual seaside hullabaloo. Hundreds of cars converge there, most of them skilfully channelled into car parks. But you have only to walk a hundred yards or so back from the sea to be free of the crowds and among saltings and sand dunes.

West Wittering village stands almost on the water's edge, but on the estuary and well back from the sea front. It is a

Canute's small daughter may be buried within the partly Saxon church at Bosham. The church is said to stand on the site of a Roman basilica.

quiet and ancient place. The district was part of the kingdom of a Celt called Commius, a Continental refugee from Julius Caesar. Coins of Commius and his three sons have been picked up in large numbers on the Wittering coast.

But it was the Saxons who gave the place the name we know today, Wihttringes, Wihthere's people. This name appears in a charter of 683, in which King Caedwalla granted St Wilfrid revenues from big areas of land. The earliest mention of the church comes about 740 in another charter, now among the Chichester diocesan records. The church you see today was rebuilt about 1180, almost certainly from the material of the Saxon church. There is a Saxon font and about forty crosses of an unfamiliar design have been carved on the flat surface of a pillar. These are the marks of medieval pilgrims, and it has been suggested that there may have been in the church a shrine to St Richard, at which the pilgrims would have worshipped.

The city of Chichester stands a little to the north-east of the harbour, and the cathedral spire is the dominating feature of the whole city. It continually bursts upon your vision. It is a comparatively new spire, built in 1861, when the fourteenth-century original succumbed to time and the elements. The second spire is a careful copy of the first. The cathedral was begun by Bishop de Luffa when he succeeded to the See in 1091. It has passed through many vicissitudes, but the spirit of Bishop Luffa's work has survived them all. His design was simple, plain, a little austere perhaps, but not bleak. In 1114 the cathedral suffered extensive damage by fire, but work went on through the twelfth century and the building was consecrated in 1184, but in 1187 it fell a victim to fire for the second time. This time rebuilding came under Bishop Seffrid II, who added the early Gothic clerestory and ribbed, stone vaulting to the nave, contrasting, though not clashing, with Bishop Luffa's Norman arcades. Purbeck stone and Caen stone were used extensively in the restoration and

The spire of Chichester Cathedral soars 277 ft above the rooftops of the city.

rebuilding and the cathedral was reconsecrated in 1199. Additions and restorations have gone on through the centuries, as the cathedral has 'grown', but the lofty vaulting and the graceful, clustered piers of the twelfth century still make the greatest and the most abiding impression.

Chichester Cathedral is a friendly though not a cosy place. Personally, I find a restfulness in the clean, uncluttered lines, the simplicity and space. It is the only English cathedral to possess a detached bell tower, built in the fifteenth century.

The city is a combination of medieval, Georgian and modern architectural styles. Roman work survives in the medieval city walls. The four main streets cross at right angles, following the pattern of their Roman predecessors, and are named after the cardinal points of the compass. At the junction stands a market cross built by Bishop Edward Story in 1501 to provide shelter for the country people who brought their produce into the city for sale. The modern name is derived from the Saxon Cisseceaster, Cissa's city. Cissa was the son of Aelle, who is generally accepted as the first ruler of the South Saxons.

On July 3, 1962, Chichester gave the world something new and revolutionary in architecture for art. This is the Chichester Festival Theatre, which is doing for the theatre what Glyndebourne has done for opera. The stage is hexagonal and nobody in the audience is more than sixty-six feet from it. Everybody has a clear view, since the roof is suspended, thus doing away with the necessity for pillars. The theatre stands in forty-three acres of Oaklands Park and cost £105,000. Its first director was Lord Olivier.

From Chichester one should really go straight to Boxgrove Priory, about three miles north-east, just before the plain begins to give way to the gentle slope of the downs. When you get there you wonder what there is remarkable about it. Grey ruins stand sadly in a green meadow, rather more forlorn than most ruins, possibly because of the contrasting lush life around. From these unhappy ruins you turn with

Chichester Festival Theatre secluded in its parkland setting.

(Above) close-up of the vaulted ceiling in Boxgrove Priory.

(Left) The chancel of Boxgrove Priory, now the nave of Boxgrove parish church. This chancel, a glorious thing, is yet only a remnant of a greater glory destroyed through the Dissolution of the Monasteries Act. The vaulted ceiling was painted in the sixteenth century by Flemish artists.

relief to the big comfortable-looking country parish church, all silver-grey flint and warm red tiles in a typically quiet English country churchyard. You push open the door, come to a full stop, and catch your breath in wonder. This is no ordinary country church. Piers, pillars and columns lead your eye upward to an exquisite vaulted ceiling, and your mind instantly goes back to Chichester.

Boxgrove was a Benedictine priory founded as a cell of the Normandy Abbey of Lessay by Robert de Haye in 1105. It was practically demolished at its dissolution in 1537, but a remnant was saved through Thomas West, ninth Lord de la Warr, whose ornate chantry stands in the church. Boxgrove parish church today is a remnant, the priory chancel and part of the nave dating from about 1210, replacing an earlier, Norman chancel. Flemish artists painted the ceiling in the sixteenth century. This chancel is considered the most important Early English building in the county after Chichester Cathedral.

South of Chichester the triangular wedge of the Selsey peninsula juts far into the sea, culminating in Selsey Bill, which is the most southerly point of Sussex. A lot of brash building has spread along the coastline here, but it could be worse. Selsey itself, not quite town but a bit more than village, has considerable charm in parts. There are quiet corners with old apple trees in gardens, and the occasional thatched roof looks perfectly natural. It is the new house next door that seems out of place. The long main street goes straight down to the shore, where it stops abruptly, as if not quite sure what to do next. As we have seen, there is nothing left of St Wilfrid's town.

The villages of the plain are often scattered. Sidlesham, for instance, stretches in several bits for over two miles down to Pagham Harbour, where it presents an exquisite water front. Climping, an attractive, two-part village split by the A27, includes some first-class thatch, and an exceptionally fine Early English church with a massive Norman tower, and it leads down to that small stretch of open coast to which I have already referred.

Scattered or compact, large or small, almost every one of these villages achieves a seclusion which is astonishing

Pagham Harbour, 698 acres, a local nature reserve since 1964. There are extensive reed beds, pools and ditches, and the area is noted for its bird life. Bognor Regis is five miles away.

considering the flatness of the land. How is it they do not stand up above the skyline in full view for miles? The reason is partly that the cottages hug the earth, and then the greatest use is made of trees and hedgerows. Nobody would ever suspect the existence of Walberton, for example, yet it is a large, cheerful-looking village, with a lot of new building, perhaps too much. Stand at the end of a cottage garden and you look over miles of meadow and field. Walk a mile over the fields and look back, and where is the village?

Several species of wildfowl breed on Chichester, Langstone and Pagham harbours. Langstone Harbour, in Hampshire, is part of the same deep inlet as Chichester Harbour, but separated by the long wedge of Hayling Island. Pagham Harbour lies just over five miles to the east. These resident wildfowl are supplemented by many thousands of visitors in winter. The dark-breasted Brent geese which winter within Chichester Harbour constitute a considerable proportion of the world Brent population. Breeding birds include redshanks, common and little terns, shelduck, shoveller duck and garganey duck. The wild, fluting cry of the redshank, 'watchdog of the marshes', echoes over mud flats and saltings at all times of the year.

In autumn evenings a peculiar and not unpleasant melancholy pervades the whole of this strange, level land. Small mists gather above the dykes and the rivulets, and along the furrows of newly ploughed fields. Then, as the last of the colour drains from the sky, through the quietness comes the whisper of many hundreds of wings beating their way down to the creeks and the flats and the wide water.

CHAPTER TWO

THE DOWNS

Even William Cobbett, who was hard to please, admired the Sussex Downs. He was one of a multitude. Probably no range of hills has been more written about, painted and photographed. Gilbert White, staying at nearby Ringmer, saw the downs as delectable mountains. Hilaire Belloc saw, from his Shipley home, what the traveller also sees as he comes into Sussex from the north, "along the sky the line of the downs, so noble and so bare". Robert Bridges loved them for their "still solitude, only matched in the skies". Kipling's lines about them are world famous, "Our blunt, bow-headed, whale-backed downs", upon whose broad, bare slopes clings the "close-bit thyme that smells like dawn in Paradise". The downs are easily the most arresting feature of the Sussex landscape, yet they occupy a relatively small area of the county. Many Sussex hilltops elsewhere are as high, and one, Black Down, is higher than any point of the Sussex Downs. But their beauty is so outstanding that all the praise lavished upon them is well merited.

There is no similarity whatever between the downs and the rest of Sussex. There are strong variations elsewhere in the county, geologically and scenically, the one depending on the other, but these differences generally merge and overlap. There is no gentle overlapping so far as the downs are concerned. They stand completely apart in splendid isolation; they look different; their soil structure is different, with a chalk foundation not to be found in any other region of Sussex; their plant life is dramatically different and very beautiful. Even the climate is different.

These striking variations are best understood through a few

Beachy Head, at 536 ft, is the highest chalk cliff on the south coast. The lighthouse began operating soon after the turn of the century. Pleasure boats from Eastbourne take visitors round it.

minutes' study of a geological map. This will show how the great chalk massive of England radiates from its heart in Wiltshire, south-west through Dorset, north-east up to the Wash, and east across Hampshire to continue in two long arms, one across Surrey and Kent, the other across the south of Sussex. The downland in the whole of this chalk massif shares similar characteristics, so that you would find more in common between the hills round Lewes and the hills round Salisbury, for instance, than you would between the Lewes hills and the Wealden meadows a couple of miles north.

From the Hampshire border the downs stretch across Sussex in a diagonal line for about fifty-five miles, coming to an abrupt and spectacular end at Beachy Head. This magnificent headland, the highest chalk cliff in the south of England, towers above the sea for 536 ft, entirely dwarfing the slim lighthouse which was built a short distance from the cliff base in 1902, to replace an existing lighthouse on the clifftop. The lighthouse on the top, called Belle Tout, came into operation in 1831, and from that lofty perch its beams shone for many miles over the Channel, but, alas, too often uselessly. Thick mists frequently creep over the Channel, hanging between the clifftop and the sea. They most effectively curtained off the beams of Belle Tout. Its sea-level successor, unhindered by the mists above, flashes a double sword of light over the water every twenty seconds. The name, Beachy Head, is thought to derive from Middle Ages French, *beau chef* (beautiful headland), but Belle Tout seems to make no sense in either French or English.

The views from Beachy Head on a clear day are superb. To the east the eye ranges over Eastbourne and the Pevensey Levels to Hastings. Immediately to the west the sheer white walls of the Seven Sisters cliffs and Seaford Head stand up out of the sea, and then you may be rewarded by a glimpse of the Isle of Wight, very far away, looking like a long, bare rock. To the north-west the downs present a broad prospect to Chanctonbury Ring and beyond, but the best views of the downs are from high points in the Weald, from which you see that incomparable line along the sky.

Both Swinburne and Richard Jefferies loved the airiness of the great headland, and poor Jefferies, up there in search of the health he never found, wrote, "it is air without admixture. If it comes from the south, the waves refine it; if inland, the wheat and flowers and grass distil it. The great headland and the whole rib of the promontory is windswept and washed with air; the billows of the atmosphere roll over it."

Thousands of summer visitors today also enjoy the delectable air of Beachy Head, but they come chiefly at week-ends. It is usually quiet enough in the middle of the week, and in winter and spring you have it to yourself. The eight-mile stretch of cliff between Beachy Head and Seaford Head is one of the Countryside Commission's 'Heritage Coasts', but it is all under some sort of protection apart from that. Beachy Head is owned by Eastbourne Council. About half the Seven Sisters cliff area is owned by the National Trust, and half by the East Sussex County Council, who have made a country park there in conjunction with the Countryside Commission. Both Council and Commission have pledged that the park will not be developed for organized recreation but that it will be left, so far as it is possible, in its natural state. Seaford Council owns Seaford Head, which is a nature reserve, and Cuckmere Haven, which separates Seaford Head from the Seven Sisters, is partly in this nature reserve and partly in the country park. In fact, the whole magnificent stretch is a single entity and no artificial barrier divides any one section from the next.

Lord Shawcross, standing on the top of Beachy Head one brilliant July afternoon in 1972, declared open the South Downs Way, which is the Countryside Commission's first combined long-distance walking route and bridle path. By far the best way to see the Sussex Downs is to walk or ride along this track, making expeditions from it as you feel inclined. I would go so far as to say it is not possible to explore the downs properly by any other means. The route mostly follows the prehistoric ridgeway track along the escarpment overlooking the Weald, and it covers about eighty miles before it reaches Hampshire, since it does not lie in a straight line over the fifty-five miles of the range.

No one knows who made this ancient track. Probably nobody did. It is more likely simply to have developed under

The cliffs between Eastbourne and Seaford are receding at an average rate of about 18 in. a year. The valleys between the arcs (the 'sisters') go first. Sometimes the walker finds that his track disappears over the edge.

A cliff fall is imminent. Falls are caused by the combined action of rain, frost and the constant pounding of the sea at the base of the cliffs.

A cliff fall along the seven Sisters cliffs. The sea soon washes away the mass of chalk, rounds the jagged lumps and finally disintegrates them. Part of the Seven Sisters area is included in the Seven Sisters Country Park and part is owned by the National Trust. A portion of the South Downs Way, for walkers only, is routed along the top of the cliffs. The bridle path takes a more northerly route.

the feet of many generations, carefully following the contours, taking the easiest way along the hilltops. In the course of time it became a highway for those people who lived here many centuries before the Celts or Romans, let alone the Saxons. It may very well have connected the settlements of the Sussex Downs with the capital of prehistoric chalkland Britain, which, perhaps, was Avebury.

Neither end of the Way has any advantage over the other as a starting point. It is a matter of convenience and personal preference. The traveller should, however, be enlightened about one thing before he starts, though no hardship or inconvenience is involved. That prospect so pleasing from northern vantage points, the long, unbroken line against the sky, is an optical illusion. The downs are cut into five blocks by four deep river valleys, which are the valleys of the Cuckmere, Ouse, Adur and Arun, and you cross them in that order if you travel east to west. Only the Cuckmere River flows freely to the sea. Each of the other three is disciplined by the town at its mouth. Newhaven bestrides the Ouse, Shoreham the Adur and Littlehampton the Arun. It is amazing that the Cuckmere should have escaped and it is only through the determined vigilance of pre-war conservationists that it has. Today it is the only river mouth free of installations from South Foreland to Portsmouth. The horned poppy and the seakale grow side by side in the shale at Cuckmere Haven, where the river loses itself in the shallows at low tide and becomes a broad band in the sea when the tide is high. In winter large numbers of wildfowl fly down from the north to these sheltered reaches. Big rafts of duck sit far out on the sea at high tide, coming in as the tide ebbs to feed among the rocks beneath the cliffs which flank the Haven on either side. Wigeon and wild geese graze the marsh pastures that stretch back from the shore. Through these pastures the river wriggles itself into an 'S', perfect meanders, and attracts a lot of attention from students and scientists. Slightly to the

On the South Downs Way near Lewes. This is the Countryside Commission's first long distance combined walking route and bridle path. It covers 80 miles in Sussex and extends a further 25 miles across the Hampshire Downs. Both Sussex Downs and East Hampshire (which takes in the Hampshire Downs) have been designated Areas of Outstanding Natural Beauty.

The meanders of the Cuckmere River. About half the area shown here forms part of the Seaford Head Nature Reserve and half comes into the Seven Sisters Country Park. The whole area is a favourite refuge for wildfowl in the winter.

east of this snake-like river another stretch of water runs dead straight towards the sea from Exceat Bridge, and first-time visitors always mistake it for the true river. This straight stretch is a man-made channel cut in 1846, and still called the New Cut. The rivers, water meadows and streams of the other three valleys also attract wildfowl in winter, but only the Cuckmere Valley provides them with a natural merging of meadow, marsh, saltings and a wild seashore.

Wild it certainly is, the only truly wild tract in the county, and it is dangerous to walk under the cliffs without taking due note of tide times and whether the cliffs are falling. At high tide the sea reaches well up the cliff face and there is no way to the top. The shore dips into shallow valleys in places, and the sea races into these declivities when the tide begins to flow, so that the too adventurous can quickly get cut off. Not infrequently they are and have to be rescued by helicopter or by boat, but they are lucky to be seen.

This under-cliff world is a tumbled no-man's land, and extends from Seaford Head to Beachy Head with only three breaks: at Birling Gap (between Beachy Head and the Seven Sisters), Cuckmere Haven, and Hope Gap, a short distance west of the Haven. It is a fascinating world and can be explored in safety provided proper precautions are taken – never go alone, and never go when the tide is coming in. It is all too easy to slip and break an ankle. Rock, seaweed, sea pools, shingle and tons of fallen cliff mingle in magnificent confusion. The cliffs are crumbling at an average rate of about eighteen inches a year, and falls vary from trickles to tons. The best way to enjoy this untouched and colourful world is to follow the ebbing tide, for then, in the pools, the crabs linger before seeking shelter beneath some overhang; the sea anemones still wave their tentacles; and the seaweeds still retain their lustre which will soon be dimmed until the flowing tide once more covers them.

The Sussex Downs today are farmed intensively on an arable pattern based on corn. This is a complete reversal of pre-war downland farming, which was almost entirely pastoral and devoted to sheep. Upon all the hills lay a thick carpet of short, springy turf, mile after mile of it, a delight to walk or sit on; and large flocks of roaming sheep cropped it, every flock with shepherd and dog. This pattern endured for centuries. The turf never felt the bite of the plough, but it was not 'natural'. The sheep created it and maintained it and W. H. Hudson called them living lawn-mowers. Had it not been for the sheep, the whole region would have become covered with impenetrable scrub, and indeed, when this extensive sheep farming began to decline, the scrub began to advance with astonishing rapidity.

But the sheep were more than turf conditioners. They created through those centuries of nibbling and manuring a very special habitat exactly right for a multitude of flowers and insects in great variety and great beauty: wild thyme, different forms of scabious, harebell, rampion and yellow rock rose, many lovely and often rare types of orchids, the chalk hill blue and Adonis blue butterflies. These are only some of the more outstanding examples of the prolific life to

(Above) Steep downland clefts like this have defied the most modern cultivating equipment. In any case the soil here would probably be too poor to bear a worthwhile crop. But such little ravines are a reservoir of chalk-loving flowers and patches of the old turf clinging to the sparse soil.

(Left) This photograph shows how arable farming has taken over from the sheep walks. The two combine harvesters are working on land which was once turf. They are cutting barley. The top of the hill in the background is also clothed with corn, but the flank immediately below has so far proved too steep to cultivate, and therefore the ancient turf still grows there.

be found only on chalk hills, and only truly flourishing when there are sheep to maintain a delicate balance of nature. Their searching teeth make short work of the young and, at that stage, succulent scrub. The turf, free of scrub, spreads and thickens. Chalk-loving flowers multiply in the turf. The flowers attract insects, which attract birds. The heart of a downland flower nestles deep in the turf and is not clipped off, and apart from the orchids, which the sheep dislike, the flower stems are wiry and the sheep avoid them. This habitat, with its treasury of life, will vanish if the newer agriculture is pursued to the exclusion of all else.

Even before the war the changing economics of agriculture were cutting down the flocks. During the war the downs were taken over by the Government for Army training. After it the Government first continued and then stepped up the drive for home food production which was an essential wartime measure. The pressure has never relaxed and is not likely to in view of the world population increase and the consequent cry for more and ever more food. In Britain this has led to a system of farming in which permanent pasture has little place.

The plough bit into the ancient turf of the Sussex Downs, and sheep, like pasture, now fit into the arable pattern. These sheep are much bigger than the native Southdown and the pasture on which they feed is the ley, which is maintained for a few years and is then ploughed to make way for some other crop. Modern grasses are far more nutritious than the old turf, and by making grass a crop in a system of rotation, it is possible to produce many more cattle and sheep. This is good farming, but it will be bad conservation if it leads to the destruction of all the old turf, the basis of such a valuable habitat. This disaster has not yet occurred, for though the remaining areas of turf are negligible compared with the expanses of the Sussex Downs as a whole, in themselves they are considerable. But it is by no means certain that these stretches will remain inviolate. Farmers give them very low priority and record them as 'rough grazing' in their returns to the Ministry of Agriculture. They are usually situated in areas which are difficult to cultivate, such as deep coombs and steep escarpments. But agricultural machinery

The West Sussex downs viewed from the Trundle. The area is an example of well-balanced estate management and comprises a mixture of arable, pasture and woodland. William Cobbett could not speak too highly of this district.

grows yearly more ingenious, and soon there will be little it cannot tackle. If all the old turf is finally brought into cultivation, a unique life structure will be brought that much nearer to extinction.

Yet farmers are understandably resentful when they are attacked for 'spoiling the downs'. After all, the land is their principal asset, and it is not reasonable to expect them to set tracts of it aside for some purpose other than farming. They are entitled to Government grants for preserving ancient field monuments, such as barrows, earth fortifications and field systems. Does not the living habitat merit equal consideration?

The transition from sheep walks to arable has been so dramatically sudden that at least one famous sheep feature of the downs has been left high if not dry. This is the dew pond.

Dew ponds were made exclusively to water the sheep, and it was one of my greatest boyhood delights to watch a flock move slowly over the scented, green-gold turf to form a close-packed ring round a little pool upon a hilltop. Today the corn grows almost to the lip of the pools, which look lonely, alien and out of place among the cultivated fields. Young walkers pause beside them and wonder how they got there, for nobody born since the war has ever seen the sheep cluster tightly round a dew pond to drink.

Dew ponds are remarkable. They never dry out, or hardly ever, and it has to be a severe drought if they do. Kipling found magic in the fact that in these little pools there was a constant supply of water in an otherwise waterless region:

> Only the dew pond on the height
> Unfed that never fails.

Why do they not fail? Some mystery has grown up around them, but without any real justification. There is no mystery, and, in the ponds, no dew worth mentioning. The shepherds never called them dew ponds. They called them shippons (sheep ponds).

There are two secrets behind the infallibility of the ponds' water supply: their site and their construction. They are always found on top of a hill or on an exposed spur, where they are perfect little catchment areas. Construction demanded meticulous care, for the pond had to be both waterproof and frost-proof. A shallow basin was first dug out, and then lined with flint and rubble, sometimes laced with mortar and sometimes followed by a layer of straw. The final layer was always a thick coat of clay brought up from the Weald by ox or horse cart. The clay was taken well over the lip of the pond so that rain could not beat under it, and it was often treated with lime, not to improve its water-retaining powers but to kill worms, whose boring would soon make the clay

"Only the dew pond on the height, Unfed that never fails." Kipling's words, and many of these little hilltop pools have still not failed, though they are no longer used by sheep, which by constant puddling kept encroaching vegetation at bay. They are sometimes used by beef stock, as shown here, but the bigger hooves of cattle tend to break down the lip of a pond.

porous and thus allow the water to drain away through the underlying chalk. Then the pond was puddled, a process which brought into play a great variety of hand-wielded implements, and sometimes, for good measure, oxen would be driven to and fro acrosss the basin. Perhaps a few buckets of water would then be tipped in to give the pond a start. After that it was simply left, and the water gradually built up, unaided.

The ponds were replenished by rain and mist, and it was the mist that kept the water level up during a dry season. Thick banks of it roll in from the Channel in the evenings and in the mornings, and when they lift they leave a glistening and a saturated world. If you are ever caught in a downland mist you will very quickly realize how great is its moisture content. You are soon wet through. The shepherds were never caught in those soaking mists. Even on the brightest day, each carried a long coat and a special shepherd's umbrella almost as big as a tent. It protected him not only from wet but also, during his meals, from sun and wind. The best-known of all the Sussex dew ponds, a very big one made in 1874 near Chanctonbury Ring, never once dried up. It was unfortunately a casualty of wartime training. I have frequently noted water in these hilltop pools when far bigger ponds in the Wealden lowlands were dry.

It says a great deal for the craft of the dew pond makers that so many of their ponds remain in good order today, though now little cared for. But they grow fewer, not because they dry out, but because they get choked by encroaching vegetation, which the hooves of the sheep used to keep at bay. Suggestions that dew ponds have a prehistoric origin can be entirely discounted. They could reckon on a life of a hundred years, but seldom more.

The downs are dominated at intervals by bold bluffs thrusting out into the Weald. Of these the most dramatic is Firle Beacon, which from some points looks almost like a peak. The view from the top is spectacular. Below, the chequer-board pattern of Wealden fields extends away to Kent and the Surrey hills, and the other way, southward, there is a great semi-circle of sea. Looking this way, you seem to be standing on the highest point of an island.

Almost as bold is a rounded hill marked on the maps Mount Caburn, but properly called 'the' Caburn. It dominates a small but arresting block of downland standing apart from the main range, two miles out in the Weald, east of Lewes. The name is probably of Celtic derivation, *Caer Bryn,* hill of the citadel, and Iron Age ramparts, dating from about 100 B.C. and strengthened about 50 B.C., crown the summit. From about 300 B.C. to 100 B.C. an open village lay acrosss the hilltop, and traces of its field systems are abundant on the surrounding slopes. An echo from Celtic Cornwall, *Caer Brane,* underlines the likelihood of the name's Celtic origin. No other Celtic name survives along the entire range, and this is surprising, since the chalk hills were thickly populated by the Celts. The Caburn is considered the most perfectly shaped hill in the whole fifty-five mile range.

Celtic Iron Age ramparts are so plentiful that sometimes you feel that every hilltop had its fort. In fact, most did. Apart from the Caburn, three stand out prominently, and one of these, Cissbury Ring, is outstanding in every sense of the word. Cissbury is by far the largest of the Sussex earthworks and, archaeologically, one of the most important in the country. It was built about 250 B.C. and covers about eighty acres, of which twenty acres are taken up by the tremendous ramparts, over a mile long. The hill it occupies is 602 ft high with wide vistas on every side. It is strategically magnificent and its construction indicates great military engineering skill. Cissbury was a fortified city and its size suggests it was a defence point for the whole of the surrounding countryside. But against what enemy? The Romans were not yet even a small cloud on the horizon. The Celts were warlike and tribal friction was common, but defences on the massive scale of Cissbury suggest a possible enemy of unusual strength. This great defensive construction was superimposed on a Neolithic settlement with flint mines, of which traces can still be seen.

The two other forts are Hollingbury and the Trundle. The Hollingbury fort is carved round the top of a hill 584 ft high, overlooking Brighton. It seems to have been occupied from about 450 to 250 B.C. and was then abandoned, but it is not known why. The Trundle (Saxon *tryndel,* a circle) was built about 300-250 B.C. on an existing Neolithic settlement, traces of which were discovered by aerial photography. The ramparts are impressive, though nothing like as massive as Cissbury. The prospect from this 676 ft hill is particularly beautiful, ranging over valleys and hills, pasture and woodland, with, to the south, a silver glimpse of Chichester Harbour.

A circular rampart on another bold bluff above the Weald encompasses that most famous of beech groves miscalled Chanctonbury Ring. The Ring is the earthwork, and the trees were planted within the raised earth circle in 1760 by a lad, Charles Goring, who inherited Wiston Estate, of which the hill was, and still is, a part. After young Goring had planted his seedlings he carried water regularly up the steep 779 ft hill to keep them moist until they took root. Charles Goring lived to a great age and saw his seedlings grow to strapping young trees. But some trees in the circle never flourished, and in 1908 it was discovered that the roots of the young trees were frustrated by the ruins of a small Roman temple. The grove is a little thinner today, and no wonder. For well over two hundred years it has survived the savage south-west gales that sweep in from the Channel over the unprotected hills, but there have been casualties and replanting has met with varying success.

In many places the South Downs Way crosses other tracks that come up out of the hills and lead down to the Weald, or just join up with the Way. There is such a crossing on Bignor Hill, about ten miles west of Chanctonbury, but this is a crossroads with a difference. The track that meets the South Downs Way on Bignor Hill sweeps up uncompromisingly from the south-west, brusquely pushes the old track out of the way, and sweeps on down the hillside on a specially built-up ramp. This is Stane Street, the great Roman highway that connected Noviomagus with Londinium. On Bignor Hill it is ninety-three feet wide in two sections, a dual carriage-

The Caburn. This isolated, 491-ft hill, standing well apart from the main range of the downs, is crowned by Iron Age ramparts built about 100 B.C. This photograph shows what the whole range of the Sussex Downs looked like before the plough-up campaign switched downland agriculture from pasture to arable.

way so to speak, with a four-foot wide bank in between. The passage of time between the Romans of Stane Street and the early users of the South Downs Way is probably about the same as that between the Stane Street Romans and ourselves. There is a delightful walk south-west down the Street for just under four miles: far from any habitation, it starts in open country, wanders into great beech and conifer woods, and ends up near a pretty little village called Eartham.

Abundant though they are, the fortified hilltops and the ancient tracks are only part of the evidence of pre-Roman populations on the downs. Though extensive ploughing has blurred or obliterated a great deal, much remains and contributes extensively to the downland scene. There are the long barrows (burial places) of the Neolithic people, the first farmers, who began arriving in this country about 3000 B.C. and spread along the chalk hills. Their flint implements are frequently turned up by the plough and may even be picked up during a walk after rain. Then there are the round barrows of the Bronze Age people, who began to come in about 1800 B.C., bringing implements and weapons of copper, which gradually gave way to bronze. The two cultures overlapped and fused. There was no definite end to the one or beginning to the other, and the introduction of bronze did not bring about the abrupt disappearance of flint.

About 600-500 B.C. a very different type of people appeared, first, probably, in small family groups, later in tribal waves. They were a lusty lot and seemed to know exactly what they wanted. But there is no evidence that they drove off or killed the existing inhabitants, and it seems more likely that they just took over. These were the Celts. They brought vastly improved agricultural methods; they replaced flint and bronze implements and weapons with iron; and their presence is stamped firmly on the chalk hills, not only by their defensive earthworks but also by their grids of square fields laid out on the gentler slopes, and long terraces

The ramparts of Cissbury, one of the biggest Iron Age forts in the country. It was built about 250 B.C., and covers 80 acres. The fort was built over the site of a large number of early Neolithic flint mines. The Neolithic people began to arrive in this country about 3000 B.C.

cut in the steeper hillsides. All are indiscriminately dubbed 'lynchets', a Saxon word meaning little hill, but the Saxon strip cultivation of the lowlands is nothing like these Celtic downland fields and terraces. There are various ideas as to their origin. The one most usually held is that the primitive Celtic plough, possessing no share, built up a raised bank at the end of a plot on the more level slopes, and that generations of one-way ploughing on the steep banks caused the soil to slip downwards, thus forming ridges. I suggest we should pause before accepting this. Many of these terraces are higher than a man is tall, and if they had been formed through a downward shift of the soil, the cultivators would have been working on solid chalk long before the banks attained the size they are. Why should not the hillsides and the slopes have been terraced deliberately? The men who built the massive ramparts of Cissbury and the even greater ramparts of Maiden Castle in Dorset would certainly have wit enough and sufficient technical knowledge to shore up terraced fields. Such terraces are still cut on Continental hillsides and are not always shored up by stone.

The most famous and the most enigmatic of all the Sussex downland echoes from the past is the Wilmington Giant. You come face to face with him at the top end of Wilmington village, a vast white figure carved on the steep flank of the down, 226 ft from top to toe, arms outstretched and holding in either hand a staff, the one on the eastern side 230 ft, the other on the western side 235 ft. In 1873 the Victorians ensured his permanence by filling him in with white bricks. But who carved him and why the staves? Some archaeologists consider him well pre-Roman, others think he is probably Nordic. The Nordic school feels its views are strongly supported by the discovery in 1964 of a Saxon buckle near Deal. It was adorned with a little figure similar to the Wilmington Giant, and carrying two spears. It is suggested

Chanctonbury. The ring is not the famous grove but a prehistoric circular earthwork. Young Charles Goring planted the trees within the ring in 1760, and afterwards carried water daily up the hill until the trees took root. He would have made his climbs roughly from the spot where this picture was taken. The beeches on the side of the hill are the descendants of the trees on top.

that both buckle and giant may be representations of the Germanic war god, Woden. Meanwhile, as always, "the Long Man of Wilmington looks naked toward the shires."

In East Sussex the downs are bold and bare, and their sweeping curves merge one into another, sinking into folds where mists gather in the evening. In West Sussex the hills are more broken and in places heavily wooded. Westward from Arundel, the Forestry Commission controls nearly 8000 acres of mixed broad-leaved trees and conifers, but mostly broad-leaves, with beeches predominating. Wildlife is rich and varied on these western, wooded hills. Walk quietly and you may catch a glimpse of deer. It will probably be fallow or roe, but may be red.

Deep in these western woodlands you come to the highest point of the Sussex Downs, Littleton Down (836 ft), but the fact has no significance because there is no view unless you climb a tall tree. However, the trees fall back from the escarpment further west, and from these points you look over the treetops to the gleaming wide water and intricate creeks of Chichester Harbour and on to the Isle of Wight. In the opposite direction, over the Weald, lie the heather and massed pines of Black Down and Hindhead.

About a mile north of the Seven Sisters cliffs the Commission has planted 1,544 acres of downland valley and hillside and it is proud of this stretch of woodland, called Friston Forest. It is a Commission showpiece. Visitors are encouraged to walk in it but cars are kept firmly out and directed to car parks well screened by trees. Ironically, Friston Forest is frequently criticized on the grounds that so many conifers disfigure the countryside and are alien to downland landscapes. At first glance one is inclined to agree with this criticism, but first glances, like patriotism, are not enough. If only critics would search out the facts before rushing to the attack, a great deal of misunderstanding and resentment would be avoided. The Friston Forest conifers are not there for keeps and were never intended to be. They are

The Long Man of Wilmington. He is an enigma. Is he prehistoric, or is he more recent, possibly Nordic? And were the two staves originally spears?

'nurse' trees to three million beeches, and they are being felled at the rate of 100 acres a year. Before 1990 the forest will be almost pure beech, and by the middle of the next century Friston Forest is expected to be one of the finest beech woodlands in the south, relieved here and there by the occasional pine, and completely open to the public.

There is a very different type of wood in a remote coomb deep in the western downs, called Kingley Vale (originally Kingley Bottom), now a national nature reserve. The floor of this valley supports a yew grove of impressive antiquity, and the steep sides are covered with younger yew trees in their prime, descendants of the ancient grove.

It is difficult to date yew trees because of their habit of merging many stems together as they grow. Nobody knows how old the old trees are. A legend says that about sixty trees were planted in A.D. 900 to commemorate a defeat of marauding Vikings. That could well have been so. Viking pirates undoubtedly sailed their long ships up the reaches of Chichester Harbour and plundered their way inland. But the legend adds that the dead Vikings were buried in four great mounds still to be seen on the top of Bow Hill, which encloses one end of the Vale. This is pure fantasy. The mounds are certainly tombs, but they are about 3,500 years old. They are Bronze Age barrows.

The stillness is cloister-like in the ancient grove. Your footfalls are silent on the thick humus built up through many centuries by the foliage fallen from the trees The canopy above is thick, the light beneath is dim. You are surrounded by strange, contorted shapes – twisted limbs, half fallen boughs that have taken root in the humus, thick writhing stems of the wild clematis, all supported by the immense girth of the tree trunks, and all seen in a greenish twilight. It is eerie at any time, but particularly at dusk and dark, and once nobody would on any account venture into Kingley Vale after daylight. E. V. Lucas, in his *Highways and Byways in Sussex*, says that Kingley Vale, "always grave and silent, is

Felling nurse conifers in Friston Forest. The felled trees are sold for wood pulp, and they are being cleared at the rate of about 100 acres a year. Friston Forest is open to the public.

transformed at dusk into a sinister and fantastic forest, a home of witchcraft and unquiet spirits."

The only towns along the whole range of the Sussex Downs are Lewes and Arundel. Lewes stands at the head of the Ouse Valley in a hollow among the downs, and Arundel clings to a hillside sloping south to the River Arun and overlooking the coastal plain.

Lewes occupies an important place in history books on account of the great battle fought on the hills west of the town in 1264, when Simon de Montfort defeated Henry III and set the country a step further on the course to representative government.

Though not much is known about the town in Saxon times, it was undoubtedly a place of some consequence, since it included two mints in the reign of King Athelstan (895-939), memorable as the first king to forge a united England under one ruler. The status of Lewes rose considerably after the Norman Conquest. For one thing, here was a point which called for immediate and strong fortification, and this task was carried out by William de Warenne, to whom the Conqueror gave the Rape of Lewes. William de Warenne built a powerful castle on a hilltop from which it still dominates the town. With this work, he began as he meant to go on. Most early Norman fortresses were constructed at first with earthworks and timber, and stone fortifications came later, but de Warenne used flint to build his castle. I was taken up to the keep when I was a small boy, and gazed with something like awe at the view, which is noteworthy even in a county renowned for views. I thought an eagle must have the same kind of outlook, for nothing could move in any direction without being seen. William, surveying the site, must have had some such thought, for he set to work to create an impregnable fortress. It was further strengthened in the early fourteenth century by a barbican which was one of the mightiest in the land. But no foe ever risked it and Lewes Castle was never engaged in battle. It was

A twilight recess in the ancient yew grove on the floor of Kingley Vale. The grove is said to be the finest in Europe. Regeneration of the old trees has clothed the sides of the valley, which is now a national nature reserve.

dismantled in 1620-21 and flints were sold to Lewes residents at 4d a load. It is now in the safekeeping of the Sussex Archaeological Society.

After about ten years of unremitting work, de Warenne and his wife Gundrada took a break in France. There they were enthralled by the famous Abbey of Cluny, and in 1077 they founded a great Cluniac monastery at Lewes, the Priory of St. Pancras, whose noble buildings included a church which rivalled Chichester Cathedral. Both William and Gundrada were buried in it. The priory also became an important centre of art and learning. But, since it depended on the mother house at Cluny, it was often frowned upon by English authority during the quarrels between England and France. The priory became the property of Thomas Cromwell at its dissolution in 1537, and Cromwell set an Italian engineer, Portinani, to demolish it, which he did with depressing thoroughness. After that the priory became a quarry. Stones were taken from it for re-use in other buildings, and now it is difficult to picture, from the few forlorn remains, the fine architecture which once graced the green meadows beside what was then the wide estuary of the Ouse. Today the railway runs where the church and cloister stood.

Despite the onslaught of modern traffic, Lewes has managed to retain much of its medieval and Elizabethan charm, which mingles easily with its Georgian grace, particularly in the narrow High Street, and the even narrower lanes which run steeply down from it to Southover High Street. Wide views constantly take you by surprise as you take this turning or that. There are fine examples of knapped flint work and timber framing. One of the High Street half-timbered houses, Bull House (once an inn), which was built in the fifteenth century and has sixteenth-century additions, was the home of Tom Paine, author of *The Rights of Man,* from 1768 to 1774. John Evelyn, the diarist, spent his boyhood at Southover Grange which was built in 1572 with stone from the ruined priory.

(Left) *The keep of Lewes Castle is built on a mound high above the town.*

(Overleaf) *"Bare slopes where chasing shadows skim." Windover Hill from the west above Alfriston.*

Lewes has two interesting museums, both run by the Sussex Archaeological Society. Barbican House, by the castle, houses the society's prehistoric, Roman, Saxon and medieval collections as well as exhibits from succeeding centuries. The other, at Anne of Cleves House, Southover, is a folk museum and illustrates Sussex life and industry, with a strong emphasis on Wealden ironwork. The house is delightful, partly Elizabethan and partly early sixteenth century.

The town's greatest claim to fame today is the spectacular display put on every November 5 by companies of Bonfire Boys. Crowds throng the town every year to see the torchlight procession, the fires and the fireworks.

Arundel, from the distance, looks distinctly continental. White, grey and red houses cling to a steep hillside which rises directly from the River Arun, and at the highest point the Roman Catholic Church of St Philip Neri stands up boldly against the skyline, while to the east, and overlooking river and valley, the grey battlemented castle towers high above the tallest trees. It is the sort of thing one grows familiar with in France. Indeed, the distant view reminds one strongly of Mont St Michel, particularly as the Church of St Philip Neri is in the French Gothic style of about 1300, though it was, in fact, built in 1870-73 to commemorate the coming of age of the fifteenth Duke of Norfolk, of the traditionally Catholic Howard family. The town does not look quite English even when you get into it. One long street climbs the hill, little streets lead off it, and houses of various age, size and shape stand cheek by jowl, usually flush with the road. It is an attractive architectural medley.

But nothing could be more English once you are in the park, all grazed pasture and lofty beeches, and a lake too. It stretches north from the castle, rising steadily, merges into the downs, and eventually rewards the walker with a panoramic view of the Arun Valley. This valley, with its hanging beech woods above the park, its broad pastures and the great hills receding on either side, has few rivals anywhere for tranquil beauty.

Keere Street, Lewes, runs down from the busy High Street and is for pedestrians only.

The castle, for all its appearance of medieval might, is nearly all late nineteenth century in thirteenth-century style. Roger de Montgomery, first Earl of Arundel, built the first Norman castle towards the end of the eleventh century, and it was considerably extended in the twelfth. This castle, which may well have succeeded a Saxon fortress, controlled the Rape of Arundel. It was dismantled after the Civil War, restored 1791-1815 and virtually rebuilt 1890-1903. The Dukes of Norfolk have owned it since 1580.

A predecessor of the Howards, Richard Fitzalan, Earl of Arundel, built the parish church of St Nicholas in 1380. It is a cruciform structure and stands on the hilltop site of a Benedictine priory. Wall paintings depict the Seven Deadly Sins and the Seven Works of Mercy.

For many centuries Arundel was a thriving port, and the Arun, largest of the four rivers that cut through the downs, is still strongly tidal far beyond the town.

Downland villages are fairly numerous, but they are nowhere plentiful, and you never feel these villages are going to explode into sprawling pink estates over the hills. They all have two things in common: they were originally built of flint, which still predominates; and they are all situated in the valleys and never on high ground. These valleys are often long but seldom wide, and therefore you do not find the spreading village greens so often a characteristic of more level country. For the same reason the villages are compact and the houses are usually grouped closely together. Greens there are, but they are small and dainty and you would certainly not play cricket on them.

With one or two exceptions these Sussex downland villages are unspoilt. Most maintain a nice balance between agriculture and tourism, and some, in West Sussex, are remote enough not to have felt the touch of tourism at all, beyond the occasional walker or the motorist content to travel along at the pace of a tractor.

The village most popular with tourists is probably Alfriston, at the head of the Cuckmere Valley, sheltered on either side by long arms of the downs. Despite the coachloads of visitors, Alfriston has retained a certain tranquillity in a way that, for instance, Widecombe-in-the-Moor, has not. In winter or in the middle of the week or at evening at any time of the year, it is sheer delight. Its 600-year-old church stands on a mound slightly apart from the long, main street, and overlooks the river and one of those small greens, called the Tye (Old English *teag*, enclosure. This word, *teag*, is also to be found as a Sussex surname, especially in long-standing downland families). It is an exceptionally large church for the downs. Most are modest, intimate little buildings, 'little, lost down churches', with demure little flattened spires on top. Alfriston is cruciform, with a tall, shingled spire, walls of superbly knapped flint – unmarred by 'improvements' or extensions – and a landmark all down the valley and far over the hills. The flints are meticulously shaped like bricks, and in the early morning or evening sunlight the walls gleam black and silver. The church is known affectionately as the 'Cathedral of the Downs'.

A very old, heavily timbered and meticulously thatched little house stands in the shadow of the church. This is the Clergy House, built about 1350, the first building to be owned by the National Trust, who bought it in 1896.

Two venerable hotels face each other across the street, the *Star*, once a hostelry for pilgrims travelling to the shrine of St Richard at Chichester, and the *George*, whose walls bear medieval paintings. The *Star* was founded in the thirteenth century, though the present building dates from about 1450.

All Sussex smuggled in the eighteenth century and Alfriston was a main smuggling centre. The whole district was held in terror by a notorious gang led by Stanton Collins, who lived in Market Cross House, now an inn. On moonless nights, knows as 'darks', clippers swept up with the tide and stood-to off Cuckmere Haven. The Collins men rowed out to them, silently took off the barrels and the bales, and either rowed back to Alfriston up the river or made their way by horse and cart through little-known downland routes. It was at this stage, if you were wise, that you would "watch the wall my darling, while the gentlemen go by". The goods were stored at Alfriston and the surrounding neighbourhood in many ingenious places until it was safe to transport them on the next leg to London. Stanton Collins and his men did the work and similar gangs elsewhere did similar work. But

(Above) The Clergy House, Alfriston, the first property to be bought by the National Trust. It was built about 1350.

(Left) Alfriston Church, the 'cathedral' of the downs. A legend says that the builders intended to place the church on the other side of the village, but each night the stones were miraculously moved. Finally, the builders were given clear and direct guidance. Four oxen lay in the shape of a cross on a little hill above the Cuckmere River, and the church was built as the oxen lay.

behind the traffic there must have been a brilliant organization, and who were the men in that?

Alfriston is not 'Alfred's town', but 'Alfric's ton', and it is pronounced All-friston. King Alfred may have had connections with the Cuckmere Valley, however. South of Alfriston, and at the end of a long lane, lies West Dean, well hidden by the trees of Friston Forest. It is an exquisite little village, and in the middle of it are the grey, medieval ruins of a big manor house and circular dovecote which is thought to stand on the site of a palace of King Alfred. Traces of the palace may remain in the manor's walls, in which, once again, meticulously knapped flints have been used. There is a little church on a hill, which was built partly in Norman times and partly in the fourteenth century, with a strange, helmet-like spire unique in the county.

There is a string of pleasant villages in the Ouse Valley: Piddinghoe, Southease, Iford, Rodmell and Kingston-near-Lewes, in that order from the south. A visitor driving down to Newhaven from Lewes on the A275 would pass each one of these villages, except Piddinghoe, and not know they were there, they are so cunningly concealed. The churches of both Piddinghoe and Southease, both twelfth century, are distinguished by round towers. The only other round church tower in Sussex, also in the Ouse Valley, is St Michael's, Lewes, built in the thirteenth century.

Kingston is snugly tucked under a ridge of down extending west towards Brighton. On this ridge, which is almost a plateau, W. H. Hudson was delighted to find the unimpeded miles of grass so like the South American pampas he remembered from early years, and he discovered that the downs offered "a thousand unimagined pleasures . . . a pleasure for every day and hour, and for every step, since it was a delight simply to walk on that elastic turf and to breathe that pure air."

On the same stretch a very remarkable shepherd, John Dudeney, educated himself while watching his flock. He was born in 1782 and started work when he was eight. He spent the few pence he earned on books and his parents encouraged him. He was lucky here, for his parents, unlike most men and women of their class, were not illiterate. His mother taught him to read, his father to write and do arithmetic. When he was 17 he got a job as under shepherd and looked after a flock of 1,400 sheep. His wages went up to six pounds a year and most of it went on books bought in the Lewes bookshops. An accident then led to his learning French. One day, reaching home after a book-buying expedition, he found he had bought, by mistake, a book in French. It was useless. But the book had cost 9d and John Dudeney could not afford to throw money away lightly. He bought two more books, a French grammar and an English-French dictionary. He studied them at night and as he walked his sheep, until finally he was able to read the book he had bought by mistake.

Dudeney then took up geometry, algebra, astronomy and Hebrew. It is one thing to carry a book, but quite another to cart about a young library. Dudeney solved this problem by digging a hole in the turf, and putting into it at night his books, slate, compasses and other items of equipment. He covered the hole with a big flint. Dudeney called it his understone library.

Presently the Vicar of Rottingdean gave him the run of the vicarage library, and after that his advancement was rapid. When he was still only twenty-two, Mr W. E. Baxter, printer and publisher of Lewes, offered him a job, and John Dudeney left his sheep, which he had never neglected during his quest for education. Eventually he said goodbye to Mr Baxter so that he could open a school, and as a schoolmaster he was held in high esteem by all social classes in an age when class distinctions were very marked. He was still teaching a few weeks before he died at the age of seventy.

The downland shepherds developed strong personal preferences for the kind of crook they used, and this led to a wide variety of crooks being manufactured in the village forges. Each forge produced its own particular crook, and its origin could be instantly recognized by a shepherd. The Falmer hook (the shepherds did not use the word 'crook') was popular because it was light and well balanced. From Pyecombe, a village on the southern slopes of Wolstonbury Hill, came a hook which achieved fame. It was familiar to every shepherd and flockmaster in the country and its name

*(*Above*) Pyecombe Forge, where the famous shepherd's crook was made. Pyecombe crooks are still made, but now not only for shepherds but also for processional use in churches and cathedrals. Some of these symbolic crooks are sent to churches overseas. The forge also produces a considerable amount of wrought iron for use in public buildings.*

*(*Left*) Harry Coppard, last of the traditional shepherds of the Sussex Downs. For over 50 years he walked his flock on the hills between Patcham and Ditchling Beacon. The flock was sold in 1951 and Harry took up gardening, for there were no more flocks to tend the way he used to do it. He died in 1963 when he was 77. His father and his grandfather walked the same hills as Harry. The crook he is holding here is a Falmer crook which he preferred to the more famous Pyecombe crook.*

lives on. Its chief characteristic was that it had a longer guide (the curly piece which twists up at the end) than any other hook. The Pyecombe forge now produces crooks not only for shepherds but also for symbolic use by bishops.

Three villages, Singleton, Charlton and East Dean, bestride the little river that flows through the Lavant Valley, where you can be sure of peace and quiet despite the nearness of the Chichester-Midhurst road. The villages are connected by a lane which not so long ago was just a track. Singleton is a picture-book village. Small cottages with thatch and pretty gardens are grouped along by-ways and round a green. There are little bridges over the stream and a pond with ducks. The nave and the massive tower of the church are Saxon, and the stone archway round the main door is covered with the strange crosses of pilgrims similar to those at West Wittering.

Singleton is the home of an open-air museum, one of the few in this country. It is well laid out on a thirty-five-acre site in a valley surrounded by beeches, and is a life-sized study in downland and Wealden social history. Ancient farmhouses and buildings have been moved bodily from their original sites and re-erected (thereby saving them from certain destruction) and Sussex harvest wagons have been carefully ranged together, ready for work, as they would have been on a farm.

Charlton, a mile to the east, gave its name to a famous hunt of the eighteenth century. The Charlton was renowned throughout Britain and indeed far beyond these shores. At the height of its splendour, it was controlled by huntsman Tom Johnson, who became almost as famous as the great men with whom he hunted, including the Duke of Marlborough. He died in 1774 and there is a memorial to him in Singleton church.

Despite its glory, the Charlton had died out by the beginning of the nineteenth century. But there are emphatic echoes of it in the village: Fox Hall, now a farmhouse, built in

Singleton, picture-book village. Cobbett stayed here during a rural ride in 1823. "I am very glad I came this road", he wrote, adding, "There is an appearance of comfort about the dwellings of the labourers all along here, that is very pleasant to behold."

1730 by the Duke of Richmond as a hunting lodge; the 'double palace', built as hunting lodges for the Duke of Devonshire and Lord Harcourt, now also a farmhouse; and Tom Johnson's cottage, standing – a little poignantly – apart, with a clear sweep of downland beyond. The story of the hunt is told on a broadsheet in the Fox Inn, which also dates from the eighteenth century, or is perhaps a little older.

Another mile or so east along the lane brings you suddenly to East Dean, with its flint and timbered cottages grouped along the lane and round a pond with a weeping willow tree, and its twelfth-century restored church on the edge of the fields. The main doorway is framed by an exquisite arch built about 1200.

Cobbett thoroughly approved of the Lavant Valley, which he passed through on his Rural Ride from London to south-east Hampshire in the summer of 1823. He records, "The lane goes along through some of the finest farms in the world. It is impossible for corn land and for agriculture to be finer than these." Not even "a really soaking day" could curb his enthusiasm. He arrived wet through at Singleton, put his coat by the kitchen fire to dry: "I have another fire and have dried my shirt on my back." Despite these tribulations, he adds, " . . . these villages are beautiful to behold . . . I saw, and with great delight, a pig at almost every labourer's house. The houses are good and warm; and the gardens some of the very best that I have seen in England."

He was a good deal less complimentary about some other regions!

The well-being so scrupulously noted by Cobbett was due largely to the progressive measures practised on the Goodwood estate by the Duke of Richmond – the well laid out farms, the comfortable cottages, and belts of timber planted for their aesthetic appeal as well as for their commercial value. The pleasant, balanced countryside of today is derived from these measures. Goodwood House itself, built of Sussex flint in the late eighteenth century, fits into the scene as naturally as the flint cottages in the Lavant Valley. Yet such countryside is vulnerable, and it is marred in places by abominably sited electricity pylons.

Westward, deep in the downs, lie the Mardens, a cluster of

small, lonely agricultural villages, built almost entirely of flint. They are unspoilt by the trappings of the tourist trade – just simple and lovely.

Under the steep north flank of the downs lies a narrow belt of land which is neither downland nor Weald. It is higher than the Weald, and, although the Weald view has begun to open out you are not yet on the chalk. It is like a shallow platform and, in fact, geologists call it the 'scarpface platform'. It is mostly light and sandy. The villages on it have all the characteristics of downland villages, and a few advance upwards along the lower spurs of the hills. Most have grown up beside lanes that do not go anywhere beyond the village, or else give way to paths or tracks that climb the down. They are therefore free of rushing traffic. There are more 'border' downland villages than true downland villages and they are lovely in an unpretentious way. Some are connected by an underhill route which can be traced the whole length of the Sussex Downs, sometimes as a track or a narrow path, sometimes a lane, and sometimes widening to a road. This route may be as ancient as the South Downs Way.

Four border villages of particular charm lie in a row under the downs near Alfriston. The most easterly, Wilmington, climbs half a mile up the lane, the last part between steep banks white with snowdrops in the spring, and emerges beside the ruins of a Benedictine priory founded in the eleventh century and in full view of the Long Man. The buildings on the site now include a small agricultural museum. The church, next door, was part of the priory and in the churchyard stands a twin-trunked yew, a thousand years old, perhaps the oldest tree in Sussex and older than church and priory.

The walls and pillars of the twelfth-century church in the next village, Berwick, are covered with murals painted by Duncan Grant, Vanessa Bell and Quentin Bell in 1942-45 after the church had been damaged by a bomb. Their setting is contemporary, pastoral Sussex. These paintings excited a lot of controversy which has never really died. I feel objections have been based largely on prejudice against any modern paintings on the walls at all, rather than against the artists' treatment of their subject. I think these paintings express the

New Testament message of compassion in a way the medieval church murals never did.

Alciston, next in line, includes one of the biggest tithe barns in England, all flint, tile and mighty timbers. There is also a fourteenth-century dovecote. Then comes Firle, both sides of a long and curving lane, with big trees overhanging and a fourteenth-fifteenth century church and a farmstead at the end. A little apart from the village stands Firle Place, ancestral home of the Gages since the fifteenth century. The old pattern of stately homes was mansion, gardens (often with terraces), lawns, shrubberies and then, naturally and without any hard line of distinction, the park. This is how Firle Place is still maintained, with the added naturalness of the park merging into downland. The original Tudor building was extensively altered in the eighteenth century, and it is the spacious dignity of Georgian architecture that meets the eye today. Firle Place is open to the public in the summer.

The eastern wall of the Caburn shelters the village of Glynde, where a remarkable man, John Ellman, farmed from 1780 to 1829. Ellman 'invented' the Southdown sheep, which became world famous. He did it by careful, selective breeding, using the unpromising rangy sheep which then roamed the downs. In agricultural circles he is known as the 'father of the Southdown'. It may also be said that the Southdown, in its turn, is the father of all the Down breeds of sheep, for Southdown blood flows strongly in them all.

Glynde Place, slightly north of the village, was built of flint and Caen stone for an iron master, William Morley, in 1569. The estate came by inheritance to Richard Trevor, Bishop of Durham, who lived in the house from 1707 to 1771, and considerably altered it. There is a splendid parkland vista.

Glyndebourne, about a mile and a half up the Ringmer road, is a by-word for quality in music and opera. The house

An underhill way at the foot of the downs is probably as old as the ridgeway (now called the South Downs Way). Sometimes it is a path, sometimes a track or a lane and in places it becomes a well-used road. This photograph was taken at the foot of Newtimber Hill.

is mostly Victorian but contains many architectural echoes of former centuries, including pre-Elizabethan panelling. In the thirties Mr John Christie built the now famous opera house in the grounds and the curtain went up on the first performance in 1934. The whole venture was widely dismissed as a rich man's fad. Whoever heard of opera on a country estate far from any city? But it quickly became clear that a new brilliance had blazed into the operatic world, and for audiences the location is part of the glory. When they stroll on the lawns during Glyndebourne's long intervals they may hear, as a temporary substitute for the singers and the orchestra, a chorus of larks in the sky.

Medieval paintings are not uncommon upon the walls of ancient Sussex churches, but they are usually too dim or too few to carry much significance. In two churches, however, at Clayton and Hardham, the paintings are so well preserved that not only can we appreciate the talent of the unknown artists, thought to have been monks from Lewes Priory, but we can also apprehend why they were done. They were not intended as adornment: they took the place of picture books with a moral for people in an age when few could read or write. There was little to read, anyway, in those days long before Caxton. The moral of the pictures is clear, and it reaches us over the centuries with startling clarity. If you were righteous you were taken up to Heaven, if you were sinful you were flung down into Hell. The pictures show serenity and blessedness, they show agony and torment, and they indicate inflexible justice, but they show no pity, mercy or compassion.

The Clayton pictures were painted in about 1150 on plaster while it was still wet. They were covered up for centuries and not discovered until 1893. That they are now to be seen again in something not too far removed from their original glowing colours is due to very skilful restoration.

The little church is a mixture of Norman and Early English with some remains of an earlier Saxon church. "There is a church," says Domesday Book, "and 23 acres of medow." The village clings to the base of the down, and brooding over everything on the crest are the two windmills, Jack and Jill, familiar to every London-to-Brighton railway commuter. Jack, a black tower mill, was built in 1876 and worked until

1908. Jill, the smaller, is a white post mill built in 1821 in Brighton. She was towed up Clayton Hill by a team of oxen and worked until 1909. About three miles west, Poynings strings itself along a leafy lane, dominated by the square tower of a flint, fourteenth-century cruciform church and sheltered by the big hills round the Devil's Dyke. Fulking, a mile further on, is distinguished by a crystal clear spring, very rare on the downs. It bubbles out from the hills to the wayside, and the fountain through which it forces its way is a memorial to John Ruskin, who loved the spot, and wanted to use the spring to improve Fulking's water supply.

Washington, under Chanctonbury, is a surprisingly large village considering that it is practically invisible until you are in it. It is also a pleasant place, with an engaging variety of houses with much flint and sandstone, winding ways and a large church once Norman but rebuilt in 1867. The A24 London-to-Worthing road used to pass close by, until it was replaced by a wide dual carriageway further off.

By no stretch of an unkind imagination could one speak of Amberley today as E. V. Lucas did at about the turn of the century. "All Amberley", he said, "is a huge stockyard, smelling of straw and cattle."

I should say Amberley is one of the neatest villages in the county. It has retained the charm of age but has banished the squalor. Thatched roofs crown flint, timber-framed and whitewashed walls, and the whole immaculate village suggests an attitude of disdain for the vulgarity and noise of the twentieth century without sinking to the silliness of 'ye olde'. It has been preserved but not mummified.

The village ends where the land drops steeply down like a cliff to the Wild Brooks in the Arun Valley. There is no doubt that Amberley stands on a platform. Rising sheer from the flat land of sedge and water meadow are the half-ruined walls of Amberley Castle. From this angle it looks grim, but it has never seen a battle. It was a fortified manor, the residence of the Bishops of Chichester, and it was built in the fourteenth century. It is privately owned. Amberley has a large church, part Norman part Early English, and it was probably begun by Bishop de Luffa, who built Chichester Cathedral.

Amberley, on the way down to the Wild Brooks in the Arun Valley. Amberley is one of the show villages of Sussex, and has a considerable amount of immaculate thatching.

A mile south, at Houghton, Charles II stopped for a drink at the *George and Dragon.* He did not dismount; it was 1651 and he was on his way to Shoreham, a ship and the safety of France. A mile west, Galsworthy chose to spend his last years at Bury, beside the Arun, and two miles west again you come to Bignor, loosely grouped round a square of narrow lanes.

Bignor is familiar to archaeologists because of its Roman villa, thought to be one of the finest stately homes of Roman Britain. It comprised an almost rectangular court about 200 ft by 114 ft, with corridors on all four sides, opening into rooms on the north, west and south, and with baths on

Winter, one of the mosaics in the Roman villa at Bignor. It probably dates from about the middle of the fourth century. It was part of a large pavement, much of which was damaged in the eighteenth century when trees were allowed to grow over it.

the east. There was also an outer court, which included a big barn and other farm buildings. The whole establishment probably covered about four and a half acres. The best rooms are paved with exquisite mosaic work, much of which retains its original brilliance. Subjects include Venus, dancing girls, gladiators, Ganymede and the Eagle, and the four seasons. Of these the figure of winter, depicted with a bare, wintry bough over his shoulder, is in perfect condition. The villa was also equipped with central heating.

Research suggests that the villa was built in the first century A.D., and rebuilt in the second, and that it was in constant occupation until the latter half of the fourth century, when the Empire was disintegrating before the Barbarians. The beautiful house was deserted when the Saxons came. Little by little it crumbled and collapsed. Debris and earth buried it and it was forgotten until one day in 1811 a ploughman turned up a bit of the Ganymede paving.

A fifteenth-century cottage, wonderfully restored, stands at one corner of the square of lanes, thatched and half-timbered, frequently used as a model by illustrators. Once it was the village shop; it is now in private occupation but is still called the Old Shop.

Graffham, under the hanging beeches of Graffham Down, is closely connected with two famous churchmen, Bishop Samuel Wilberforce and Cardinal Edward Manning. Wilberforce was Bishop first of Oxford (1845) and then of Winchester (1869) but he also had an estate at Graffham. He planted a clump of trees on Duncton Down, and this, of course, was instantly dubbed the Bishop's Ring. As such it is marked on the map. The Bishop is buried in Graffham churchyard.

Manning as a curate served the two parishes of Graffham and Lavington. Eventually he became rector, then Archdeacon of Chichester and ten years later transferred his allegiance to the Church of Rome. The scandal was terrific. Manning went on. Within fourteen years he was Archbishop of Westminster and by 1875 he was a cardinal.

The village has grown through the centuries beside a long, winding lane which ends at the church with the hanging woods a few yards on. The church was virtually rebuilt in 1874-86 as a Wilberforce memorial. Some Norman work was incorporated, and it is likely that a church stood on the site before the Normans came.

Richard Cobden, the unrelenting Victorian free trader, was born at nearby Heyshott, which is about as scattered a village as you are likely to find, yet is somehow held together by a semi-wild common. Cobden worshipped in the church and a plaque draws attention to the fact. The church has stood on its mound at about the centre of Heyshott since the thirteenth century. There is some nineteenth-century work, but mercifully it has been done with taste.

Then you come to the Hartings. There are three, South, East and West. The main village is South Harting, which Lucas considered "the most satisfying village in all Sussex". A long and wide central street with buildings of great variety from many centuries is dominated by a large church with a 130-ft spire clad in copper, which accounts for the greenish light it reflects. Most of the church was built early in the fourteenth century, but it seems likely that a church has stood where the present church stands since St Wilfrid brought Christianity to Sussex. Eric Gill carved the tall, slender cross in the churchyard which is the village war memorial. Stocks and whipping post immediately outside the churchyard are still in excellent working order.

A remarkable house called Uppark stands on top of a 350-ft hill south of South Harting. It was built of red brick in about 1690 and most of the exterior has never been altered. The interior is nearly all eighteenth century and the rooms, decorated and furnished mainly between 1750 and 1770, retain many original flock wallpapers, damask curtains and other textiles and fittings. One of Uppark's owners, Sir Henry Fetherstonhaugh, brought Emma Hart (later Lady Hamilton) to Uppark for a year, and visitors can see the table on which she is said to have danced. H. G. Wells's mother was housekeeper at Uppark and Wells described his boyhood there in his autobiography. The house is now owned by the National Trust.

On the southern slopes Findon has so far successfully evaded the embraces of Worthing, but for how long? All farmers know this village through its annual September sheep fair.

There are four quite unspoiled border villages where the downs slide gently down to the coastal plain. These are Slindon, Clapham, Patching and Burpham, and each is all of a piece. St Wilfrid used to visit Slindon to enjoy its beauty, and the downs round this village were the first of "the great hills of the South Country" that Belloc knew, for here he spent his childhood. Slindon House was a palace of the Archbishops of Canterbury, and Stephen Langton, who had much to do with Magna Carta, died there in 1228. He is commemorated by a plaque in the church, which stands

*(*Above*) Weaving a wattle hurdle on a Patching woodland work site. These hurdles are made of cleft hazel rods, and at each end of the hurdle they have to be given a deft twist round a strong, uncleft rod. If this is not done properly, the cleft rod will split.*

*(*Right*) The view from Duncton Hill looking north over the Weald. The low plain here is a narrow belt and the fields are smaller than the fields of the plain further east.*

where a church has stood for over a thousand years. The present church has developed from an eleventh-century building but some Saxon work remains. Inside there is an oak carving of an early Tudor knight, probably Sir Anthony St Leger. The name does not matter now; what does matter is that this carving, the only wooden effigy in Sussex, was done

Halnaker Mill. It was the subject of one of Belloc's best-known poems when the mill was in danger of collapse. It was built about 1750, was restored in 1934 and again in 1955. The name is pronounced Hanaker and is said to be derived from 'half an acre'.

by an artist of great talent. Sincerity, insight and intuition are evident in it, and you sense the authenticity of the strong nose and chin, the downturned, determined, slightly sardonic mouth, the neat, bobbed hair. Who was this sculptor of such brilliance?

Clapham and Patching are companion villages separated by the A280 road, from which each village stands back. A track at Clapham suddenly takes to the woods and comes to a full stop by the church, originally Norman, in a small clearing.

The woodland lanes of Patching were once lined with hurdle-making enterprises. One remains, the Kinnard workshop in a woodland clearing. Kinnards have been making hurdles in Patching for over three hundred years: the cleft hazel wattle hurdles with which the downland shepherds folded their flocks at night. Neither shepherds nor hurdle makers used the term 'wattle': to them the hurdles were 'flakings'.

No hurdle-making business today could exist on orders from farmers. The Kinnard workshop once made 150 dozen hurdles every year for the Findon sheep fair alone, and farmers ordered fifty dozen at a time. Now the fair demands nine or ten dozen and the farmers order about eleven dozen. But there is a growing demand from the parks and gardens departments of big towns, particularly the resorts. Private householders buy the hurdles for fencing, horticultural concerns buy them for windbreaks, and wattle gates are made in frames of oak.

Burpham stands at the end of a three-mile winding lane that goes no further. Down a steep bank immediately beyond are the Arun and its meadows, and southward spreads the plain. Over the river the crenellated profile of Arundel Castle breaks the skyline romantically. A huge mound of some twenty acres was almost certainly fortified as a defence against the Danes when Burpham was a Saxon village. The church (1160-1220) includes beautiful stone vaulting over the chancel. Apart from that, Burpham is not distinguished by anything in particular, but is idyllic in general. Such refuges are precious.

This photograph, taken from Windover Hill, shows the steep rise of the downland north escarpment in striking contrast with the level fields of the low Wealden plain. The downland track in the foreground is part of the prehistoric track now called the South Downs Way.

CHAPTER THREE

THE WEALD

What is the Weald? This is more easily asked than answered.

Geology text books too often convey the impression that it is a great bowl of a valley between the North and South Downs. This is far too much of a simplification. A vast dome once rose where the Weald lies now, like an inverted pudding basin. Bit by bit it was worn away until only stumps of the rim was left: the two chalk ranges, north and south. To that extent the text books are accurate enough. But the process of wearing down was very uneven, for some of the strata were harder than others. The inconsistent erosion and the different types of soil have provided a very wide diversity of scenery, level pastures and marshlands, long and high ridges, tumbled hills, and valleys with a corresponding diversity of vegetation.

There are definite geological regions, but they overlap, often extensively. Sometimes one geological type even drives a corridor through another, and occasionally you find an 'island' with the characteristics of one area slap in the middle of an area where the general characteristics are entirely different. So anybody who tries to describe the Weald region by region is asking for trouble, as many geologists have discovered. Yet the variety of the Weald is so great that something of the sort must be attempted.

The bulk of the Weald lies in Sussex, extending into Kent and Surrey and, to a lesser extent, into Hampshire. The Sussex Weald is at its widest towards the east where it is about twenty-five miles broad, and it runs the length of the county from Kent to Hampshire, about eighty miles.

Very roughly, the Sussex Weald may be divided into four

regions: the north-west region; the forest ridge; the south-eastern forest ridges; and the low clay plain.

The Romans knew the Weald as a wild and hostile place and they called it Silva Anderida. They drove one main highway across it which the Saxons later named Stane Street (Stone Street). They built a number of secondary roads, probably for carrying out iron from mines worked by the Celts. They also built posting stations, but in all the wild region they established no main centre. It was the tough, rough and unsophisticated Saxons, with their hefty if clumsy implements, who began the systematic settlement and cultivation of the great wild, which they called Andredsweald. The Venerable Bede (A.D. 673-735) called the forest Andred's Weald, and 'Andred' had probably been taken over from the Celts. There may be an association with the Roman 'Anderida', but it would be unwise to assume this. The Anglo-Saxon Chronicle estimates the extent of "the great wood which we call Andred" at about 120 miles east to west and about thirty broad.

Big roads from London cut through the Weald on their way to the coast, alien things, belonging to no countryside. Yet even on these fast highways you see enough to realize that you are passing through a land of very great interest though speed denies you the time to appreciate its beauty. If, however, you strike off the main roads, east or west, in an astonishingly short distance you find yourself travelling along small winding lanes, and on many of these two cars can pass only with great difficulty. Before the war a good half of these lanes were not made up and some still are not. Depending on which part of the county you are in, they may take you over heathland, through forest with the trees meeting overhead, or between meadows and small arable fields. They link together villages and hamlets, and it is possible to motor through the length of Sussex, east to west, and scarcely touch a main road except to cross it. On such a journey, of course, haste must be discounted.

All the villages and hamlets in the Weald, except those on the major roads, have one thing in common: they seem to have grown there, like the trees. This is not just a flight of fancy; it contains an element of truth. Through the centuries,

In all the regions of the Weald there is an intricate pattern of winding lanes. This lane, between Balcombe and Ardingly, is a typical example. Many are much narrower.

villages and nature in the Weald have fused, each depending on the other and both together building up a particular kind of countryside. First, the clearing in the forest, the modest homestead and the huts, both of the timber ready to hand; presently the church, a bigger homestead, a bigger clearing, and huts replaced by substantial cottages. Farms gradually grew larger, cottages more numerous; the forest slowly thinned, drainage dried the bogs.

The Saxon origin of Wealden villages is clearly proclaimed by their names, which indicate the kind of sites on which they were situated. Repeatedly you find a Saxon prefix or

suffix to a village name. For instance, hurst, the Saxon *hyrst,* a wood (Fernhurst). Or *ham,* lowland meadow (Hailsham); or *ton,* homestead or village (Warbleton). Moreover, practically every village is mentioned in the Domesday Book.

One must, however, curb one's imagination a little in establishing original Saxon sites through names, for though the name may be the same the place may have been somewhere else, though usually not far off. An ancient church some distance from its village is a pretty sure sign that the village has moved. The older village would have been clustered round the church.

For centuries little impact was made on the great wild. Saxon chief made war on Saxon chief. The Danes came. The Normans came. Meanwhile, the Saxon husbandman continued to drive his hogs into the forest. He felled a tree or two when necessary, to extend his clearing for more crops or to provide himself with timber for a new building. He got up at dawn, he went to bed at dark, and the slow years passed. But in the thirteenth century an ancient Wealden industry, half-forgotten, was re-introduced into the forest. It was to have tremendous consequences on Andredsweald, which, in the end, it destroyed. This was the production of iron.

The chief industry in the Weald has always been agriculture, but for a time iron was a very close rival. Indeed, the Wealden iron industry was of major national importance and it was the precursor of the industrial revolution. Historians have never attached enough significance to this industry, which was most concentrated in East Sussex and which changed the landscape more dramatically in less than two centuries than anything had done in the previous thousand years. Its life as a major industry lasted from the thirteenth to the eighteenth century and the peak years were the sixteenth and seventeenth centuries.

Wealden iron was mined by the Celts long before the Romans arrived. The Romans continued and expanded the industry, driving roads into the jungle to the quarries and

(Pp104-105) *The Weald from Ditchling Beacon. Ditchling village is in the middle foreground.*

Working model of a hammer mill, built for a Wealden iron industry exhibition at Bateman's, Burwash. These hammers, weighing half a ton or more, were worked by a wheel driven by water from specially constructed lakes; hence the term 'hammer ponds'. The model was made by Mr Jack Smith, Burwash Weald.

furnaces. Mining lapsed with the coming of the Saxons, and the Domesday Book records only one iron mine, near East Grinstead. There are few records concerning the revival of the industry. But in 1266 Henry III made a grant of a penny on every load of iron taken to Lewes. References are plentiful after that, and eventually the Weald became the nation's major source of iron, and iron masters became wealthy men.

The Celtic, Roman and early medieval methods of smelting were simple and not very efficient. Layers of charcoal and iron ore were built up into a mound three or four feet high over a stone hearth. The mound was covered with clay and ignited, and the fire was kept going by bellows worked by foot. After a few days, iron supple enough to be worked was

This is a well-known fire-back, housed in the Anne of Cleves House Museum, Lewes. It is dated 1636 and pictures a Brede iron founder named Richard Lennard with his dog, implements and products of his trade.

recovered from the hearth. It was beaten into rough ingots called blooms, and the furnaces were called bloomeries. But iron was seldom if ever completely extracted from the rough lumps which held it, and with the coming of more efficient methods it was often found more profitable to return the old offal to the new furnaces than to mine for fresh ore, for there was so much good iron immediately to hand in the 'cinders'.

New techniques came into operation toward the end of the fifteenth century. They were not developments of the existing Wealden bloomeries. They came from the Ardennes of northern France, and they involved the use of water

An iron master's family. The life-size models were made for exhibition on the Wealden iron industry at Bateman's, Burwash. Bateman's, later the home of Rudyard Kipling, was built for an iron master in 1634. The models were made by Mrs Betty Sutherland and her family, of Bateman's. The clothes were made by Miss Ash, wardrobe mistress for the Eastbourne Shakespeare Society.

power. Just as the great wheels of water mills were used to turn flat stones for grinding corn, so now they were used to work bellows for the blast furnaces and hammers for the forges. The bellows could be twenty feet long or more and the hammer might weigh half a ton.

William Camden, the sixteenth-century historian, explains

that "diverse brookes in many places are brought to run in one channell, and sundry meadows turned into pooles and waters." Thus the term 'hammer pond', which often puzzles visitors to Sussex, and even local residents. These hammer ponds are liberally scattered throughout the Weald. Once they were centres of industry and noise; now they are quiet, sequestered retreats where wild fowl come.

The new blast furnaces demanded a tremendous amount of timber to provide charcoal fuel. But the timber was there for the taking on all sides, and the forest was rapidly decimated. It was found profitable to manufacture large quantities of cannon not only for home defence but also for export. The Admiralty acidly pointed out that so much timber was being burnt to cast guns that presently there would be no more left to build ships. Sir Walter Raleigh complained that whereas one English ship had been able to beat ten Spanish, "now by reason of our own ordnance we are badly matcht one to one". Restrictive statutes had little effect: the felling went on.

Glass-making centres at Wisborough Green, Kirdford and Loxwood also demanded furnaces and therefore accelerated the wholesale murder of the forest. Eventually shortage led to exorbitant fuel costs, and this problem was only solved by transferring the industry to the North and the Midlands, where it was found possible and less expensive to smelt iron in conjunction with the developing coal mines. The first of the new-style Wealden furnaces was built at Hartfield in 1497. The last to close was at Ashburnham in 1809.

Various attempts were made to revive the industry. The last was as late as 1857 at Wadhurst, possibly the most important of all the iron-smelting centres. Mines were opened at Snape Wood in August but the ore had to be sent to Staffordshire for smelting. It was a valiant but forlorn effort and the mines were abandoned just over a year later in September 1858.

The Weald in its days of iron production has been called the earlier black country of England, but this is misleading. The Weald was cleared of its trees, the furnaces blew, the hammers rang, but there was never anything like the frightful grime, soot and squalor of the Victorian industrial centres.

For one thing, the industry was on a smaller scale, and for another there is a great difference between wood smoke and coal smoke. The end of the Sussex industrial age left no ugly slag heaps or mounds of rusting metal. It left a series of placid lakes and a bare landscape. Agriculture and nature stepped quietly in, and though wild Andredsweald has gone the Weald today is nevertheless again one of the most richly wooded districts in the country, so that Kipling could write about

> . . . the deep ghylls that breed
> Huge oaks and old, the which we hold
> No more than Saxon weed.

The North-West Region

The north-west corner of Sussex still retains something of a primeval nature. The hand of man has rested lightly on it. There are large tracts of sandy heathland and pinewood which have never felt the bite of the plough. Bracken and heather used to be cut for livestock bedding and for thatch, and stock found some grazing on the rough grass that grew among the heath. Cultivation has gone no farther than that. This light touch, however, had a very important effect. It was enough to maintain a balance between the bracken and the heather and to keep down the scrub. But such small-scale farming is no longer practised, and the consequence is a great upsurge of the bracken, which, if uncontrolled, will choke all other vegetation, to be smothered, in its turn, by scrub. But Sussex is cared for by a number of alert amenity societies, including the Sussex Trust for Nature Conservation, which has become expert in preserving the balance of open tracts once preserved through the commoners and their stock.

In this half-wild region, Sussex reaches its highest point, Black Down, 919 ft above sea level. Black Down is part of a big sandstone massif which also includes Hindhead across the Surrey border and extends into Hampshire. The heath commons and the woods stretch south from the massif, interspersed with patches of pasture, almost down to Midhurst and the Rother Valley, and then further south again, nearly to the downs. It is superb country, quite quiet, with sweeping views, and the only way to see and feel its beauty is to walk. Mercifully, there are abundant opportunities for doing so.

Tennyson, who lived at Aldworth House on Black Down, loved the spacious, unrestricted miles and the vistas.

> You came and looked and loved the view
> Long known and loved by me,
> Green Sussex, fading into blue,
> With one grey glimpse of sea.

Cobbett reacted differently. Land not put to some form of agricultural use always upset him, and he never minced his words about his feelings. "I have never", he wrote, "seen the earth flung about in such a wild way as round about Hindhead and Black Down."

There is a handful of villages dotted about this north-west corner of the county, all beautiful, all half-hidden by trees —Fernhurst and Henley, Lurgashall, Lodsworth and Stedham, all unspoilt and not overrun by traffic. One minute you are looking for them, wondering where they can be, and the next you are there. You might have stumbled upon them out of the forest. Northchapel and Rogate are just as lovely but lack the quietude, since they are sliced by main roads. Both Fernhurst and Lurgashall are built round large greens, each on a plateau, and the plateaux were obvious places for clearings. Deer lie up in the thickets, and you may see buzzards in the sky.

The capital of the area is Midhurst, aptly named — the town in the middle of the wood. It is a mellow place with a prosperous air, partly warm red bricks, partly black oak timber framing, and of these venerable timber-framed houses the fifteenth-century *Spread Eagle Hotel* is outstanding. Cobden was a scholar at the seventeenth-century grammar school and Wells a student teacher.

The best way to enter Midhurst is from the east, through Cowdray Park. It is a beautiful park, with lake, green and rounded hills, magnificent oaks and beeches, and the ruins of

In the land of the western heaths. View from Ambersham Common, where the heather and bracken on sandy soil almost meet the turf of the downs.

Cowdray House, once one of the finest houses in the land. It was gutted by fire in 1793 and never rebuilt. It is now only a shell, but the grace and splendour of its lines remain. Cowdray was built in the reign of Henry VIII and came into the possession of Sir Anthony Browne, the first Viscount Montagu. The last Montagu, the eighth Viscount, was drowned a week after the house was burned, thus calling to mind the Curse of Cowdray. Sir Anthony was given Battle Abbey at the Dissolution of the Monasteries, and the monks got short shrift at his hands. One of them, preferring an eye for an eye to turning the other cheek, declared, "By fire and water thy line shall perish."

Eastward the Weald widens. The downs fall back to the south-east, the high land and the Surrey border veer away north-east. Petworth, just over five miles east of Midhurst, occupies a point where the high north-west begins to slope down to the low plain. The land falls gently down to the River Rother and Duncton, and then the chalk hillside rises sharply. It is a tranquil prospect of green pasture and, in high summer, of gold and flaxen corn. Petworth is a small, snug and ancient town, with winding lanes, one of them still cobbled, and a much restored, fourteenth-century church standing on the site of a Saxon predecessor. The church tower once supported a splendid spire, built in 1827, a familiar landmark for miles round until 1947, when it was discovered to be insecure and was taken down.

But Petworth is most noted for Petworth House with its 738-acre park. The great house faces west, with its back to the town, and its front is 320 ft long. It represents a wholesale rebuilding in 1688-96, by the sixth Duke of Somerset, of a thirteenth-century manor house. In 1750 it passed to the Wyndhams, one of whom, the third Lord Leconfield, gave it to the National Trust in 1947. The house contains a superb collection of paintings, including many by Turner, who was a frequent visitor to the house. The grounds

Fernhurst. Lanes and paths lead to a green with the church at one corner and cottages round the sides. Black Down, 919 ft, the highest hill in Sussex, is less than two miles off.

were designed by Capability Brown in about the middle of the eighteenth century, and a herd of red deer roams the park.

Throughout the county you will find references to Sussex marble. This puzzles visitors, who are apt to greet any mention of such a material in such a region with scepticism, which, however, is misplaced. Sussex did produce stone always described as marble, and it was used fairly extensively in churches, particularly for fonts, but you sometimes find it also on the floors of old houses. It was quarried in some quantity in the Petworth area and is sometimes called Petworth marble. It ran in seams through the Wealden clay, usually 20 to 30 ft below the surface, and it was last quarried in 1880 at Kirdford, about four miles from Petworth.

The 'marble' is a form of limestone consisting of massed fossilized shells of the freshwater snail, *Viviparus paludina.* When polished it takes on a pleasing greenish-grey lustre. The font in Kirdford church is of this Sussex marble and is dated 1620. The paving of the church porch is of Sussex marble slabs and the floor of the *Half Moon Inn* is also partly of marble.

Kirdford today is the centre of a very different kind of industry, a big co-operative fruit-growing enterprise established in 1926 when farmland in the area was about twenty pounds an acre and farming all over Britain at almost its lowest ebb ever. This enterprise was one of the earliest examples of British co-operative farm production, the importance of which is now so frequently stressed. Its orchards have invested a big area with its own particular character, and this includes not only Kirdford but also Wisborough Green, a village with a very big green and a very tall church spire. Cricket on this green on a sunny day forms a memorable picture.

About here the low clay plain curls round to the north-east, cutting between the sandy north-west region and the sandy forest ridge, and in doing so ceases to be either low or plain. It climbs, it becomes broken, and from its eminence fine prospects can be enjoyed. In this respect it is not unlike either the north-west or the forest ridge, but in other respects it is markedly dissimilar. There is a certain

Lurgashall. A blissfully quiet village round a green, almost at the foot of Black Down. Tennyson went to church at Lurgashall.

One of the wilder tracts of the Wealden north-west. Iping Common, between Midhurst and Petersfield.

tackiness about the soil, which in hot weather becomes cracked and in wet weather sticky. Also, in place of a preponderance of pines and beeches, there is a large proportion of oaks, of which you may admire outstanding examples on Plaistow green.

Where the clay belt gives way to the lighter soil on the east stands Horsham.

The Forest Ridge

Just as Midhurst is the natural capital of the West Sussex heaths, so Horsham and East Grinstead are the natural capitals of the forest ridge, Horsham of the western end, East Grinstead of the east. Though well within the London commuter radius, each has a life and soul of its own, and neither, so far, is overshadowed by the nearby Crawley new town.

Horsham is now universally mispronounced. Hor-sham, we say, whereas it should be Hors-ham, an enclosure or meadow where horses were kept. Even today, despite the bustling traffic, you have a feeling in Horsham that you are in a place for which space has been made by clearing trees. The impression is strengthened by the approaches, all of which are wooded, very heavily on the south and east.

The heart of Horsham is the Carfax, and the only other town in England with a carfax is Oxford. The name probably comes from the Latin *quadrifurcus,* four streets, though more streets than that now open into Horsham Carfax. The Carfax in its turn opens into a tiny Market Square, which is bounded by the Town Hall, a rather grim nineteenth-century building with turrets on it. It is flanked on either side by a narrow, inconspicuous passageway, easy to overlook and with nothing to tempt you in. It would be a great mistake not to pass through, however, for on the other side you find yourself suddenly in a wide, secluded avenue, easily the most beautiful part of the town. E. V. Lucas wrote of it that "there is in England no more peaceful and prosperous row of venerable houses". This is the Causeway, a wide cul-de-sac bounded at the further end by the parish church, with a shingled spire soaring 230 ft into the sky. There are 50,000 shingles on the timber framework of that spire, which has an engaging wiggle on the top. The church is part Norman, part Early English, but nineteenth-century 'restoration' swept away some architecture which might have been better retained. Under the tower is a memorial slab to the poet Shelley, who was born not far off at Field Place.

Horsham is a mixture of the ancient, the not so ancient and the modern. Surprisingly, it is not registered in Domesday but it had become an important centre by 1236, when it was referred to as a borough. It retained that status until 1885, but unofficially, for it was never granted a charter.

The countryside round Horsham used to be the centre of

an industry exclusive to Sussex: quarrying for a particular kind of stone which, suitably, bears the name of the town. Horsham stone is a calcareous sandstone, silver-grey and frequently rippled. It was widely used for roofing, but sometimes also for floors and paving, and it is variously called Horsham tiles, stone, slate or slabs. As it weathers, it attracts little clumps of amber moss. Visitors to Sussex invariably exclaim with delight at these lovely roofs and the massively timbered walls. Massive they had to be to hold up such weights of stone. One Horsham slab may weigh half a hundredweight.

Horsham serves a circle of villages and isolated farms as it has served them for centuries – compact, unspoiled villages like Warnham, Rusper and Rudgwick, Slinfold, Nuthurst and Barns Green, with Itchingfield scattered along upland lanes, un-urban places where men come home at night from the fields. Itchingfield is distinguished by a tiny fifteenth-century architectural gem, a half-timbered priest's house in the churchyard, and a big red brick public school, Christ's Hospital, the Bluecoat School, founded in London by Edward VI in 1552 and moved to Sussex in 1902.

The forest ridge stretches east of Horsham for about twenty miles. East and south, forests run into one another, St Leonard's, Tilgate, Worth and Balcombe Forests, miles of superb woodlands, substantial reminders of the ancient jungle, though practically all have been replanted systematically. They are mostly privately owned, but they are threaded with footpaths and narrow lanes. Some of these pass along the banks of broad lakes which more often than not were the hammer ponds of the iron industry. North of the trees lies Crawley, designated a new town in 1947 when the population was 9000. Over Crawley there now hangs a sinister question mark. How much of Sussex is this young town going to gobble up?

The Causeway, Horsham. This is a beautiful cul-de-sac *leading from the Carfax to the church. It is wide and airy but also secluded. There is great variety among the houses, with lovely examples of seventeenth, eighteenth and early nineteenth-century architecture, but a distinct sense of harmony too.*

(Above) The Mill House, Balcombe. Such idyllic scenes are common among the woodlands of the Forest Ridge.

(Right) Just messing about in a boat where the iron furnaces blew. A lake in Balcombe Forest.

The trees continue eastward far from the actual boundaries of the forests, only slightly less dense and in some places just as thick as the forest itself. The land rises steadily and becomes very broken, with steep grassy valleys among the trees and splendid views over the varied landscape to the downs, which are now much more distant and are seen as that entrancing long line across the sky.

In this high, thickly wooded country lies Wakehurst Place, near Ardingly (pronounced Arding-lie and not -lee). Wakehurst is owned by the National Trust, who have let the 462-acre estate at a nominal rent to the Ministry of Agriculture for the use of the Royal Botanic Gardens, Kew. Wakehurst is a household word in horticultural circles on account of its world-wide collection of trees and shrubs, but it is also a place of great natural beauty. The native oaks, pines and beeches have not been cleared to make way for the imported specimens. These grow happily among the established vegetation, but there are also big tracts of typical Wealden woodland, and perhaps partly sprung from natural regeneration from the old Weald. It would not be true to say that here nature is left alone. If it were, nobody would get through except with an axe. But restraint is discreet and extends to little more than checking undergrowth. Here, if anywhere, you can catch an echo of the ancient wild as it was on this high, northern ridge.

The soil on the ridge is sandy, with bold outcrops of sandstone rock, of which there are excellent examples at Wakehurst. In one place the roots of yews and beeches claw over a long line of big rocks to reach the sustenance of the earth below. The most dramatic outcrop is near Eridge, on the eastern boundary of the county, where the rock is sheer enough and high enough to provide practice for budding climbers. The most amazing, however, is Big-on-Little near West Hoathly, where a very large, rounded rock is perched, apparently with great insecurity, upon a smaller rock, also rounded. Cobbett wanted to know "how came this big on little", and in his day there was none to tell him that nobody cast up Big upon Little but that gradual erosion around just left them like that.

In the woods of Wakehurst Place, Ardingly. Native trees of the Weald, particularly oaks and beeches, can be seen here growing in a more or less wild state. The collected specimens of trees and shrubs from many parts of the world are planted among the native trees, but there are large areas in which the vegetation of the old Weald grows exclusively. This picture shows such an area. The 462-acre estate is an 'annexe' of the Royal Botanic Gardens, Kew.

West Hoathly is perched high on the ridge round a triangle of lanes. You reach it unexpectedly, finding yourself suddenly in the middle of the village with the church one side and the *Cat Inn* the other, and at this point you have little sense of altitude. But just walk through the churchyard. The ground drops away before your feet with precipitous suddenness and your eye travels over woodland, valley, farm and steeple to the far horizon where the downs rise up to meet the sky. Some of the church dates from 1090 and its shingled spire is a landmark for many miles.

West Hoathly's great treasure is a fifteenth-century Priest House, a perfect example of massive, timber-framed walls supporting a roof of Horsham slabs. The Priest House is now a museum, in the care of the Sussex Archaeological Trust, but it is a museum with a difference. It is arranged as a dwelling house, and anybody walking in from the eighteenth or nineteenth centuries would feel reasonably at home in these surroundings, and would enjoy the vases of cottage flowers from the cottage garden outside.

A narrow and highly scenic road goes on eastward from West Hoathly and in three miles reaches Ashdown Forest, where, despite its name, the trees thin out. You do not walk *in* Ashdown Forest, you walk *on* it, for it is now more moorland than woodland, with splendid vistas over heather and bracken, dramatic clumps of pines, boggy valleys, streams and rough pasture. There is also a marvellous range of wild flowers, some of them rare, like the marsh gentian. It is due to the determination of the Ashdown Forest commoners that we can still enjoy this open, breezy tract.

Commoners have had rights on Ashdown Forest certainly since the time of the Normans and probably before. Changes of ownership meant little to them. In 1372 Edward III gave the forest, then 14,000 acres, to his third son, John of Gaunt, who developed its attractions as a hunting ground. It

The fifteenth-century Priest House at West Hoathly. This is a first-class example of timber-framed walls with Horsham slab roof. The house is now a folk museum.

The open, breezy heights of Ashdown Forest are frequently broken by lonely clumps of pines. This is Camp Hill, 650 ft above sea level. The view from this point takes in a wide belt of the Weald to the downs.

remained part of the Duchy of Lancaster for three centuries, but new owners with different ideas appeared in the seventeenth century after the Restoration. They began to split up the forest and enclose it, but they reckoned without the commoners who found themselves banished from their woodlands and grazing, and tore down the fences. It was a long fight but in the end they won.

In 1693 a Royal Commission awarded 6,400 acres for the use and enjoyment of the commoners and that is the extent of the open land to this day. A map was drawn up showing

Fire is the great peril to Ashdown Forest. Every spring and summer, despite appeals for care, tracts of the forest are blackened and many birds and small animals die. Fire-fighting services are constantly maintained and an out-break can be reached within minutes. But dry bracken and gorse burn very quickly: a few moments after this picture was taken the area in the foreground was alight.

who had rights over what. From this map the Ashdown Forest we know today is still clearly recognizable, though some references on it induce wistful feelings. What on the map was charmingly marked 'a green ride' is today the reeking A22 London-Eastbourne highway. But most of the region remains mercifully peaceful, even though week-end visitors increase every year, not surprisingly, since London is only 35 miles off. They bring another kind of danger – fire. Outbreaks occur every spring and summer and are almost always caused by thoughtlessness, usually a thrown-down cigarette end not properly stubbed, or a smouldering match. The little act of carelessness often has very serious consequences, in particular the deaths of small birds and animals.

Unlike most common land, Ashdown Forest is administered by a board of conservators under a succession of Acts of Parliament. Cobbett, of course, had no time for the place, which to him was "verily the most villainously ugly spot I ever saw in England".

Older cottages on and near the forest are usually built of sandstone, dug up or simply picked up within yards of the site. Nearby villages also include attractive sandstone buildings. Forest Row, the 'capital' of the forest, is a mixture of ancient and modern. It stands on the banks of the River Medway at the junction of the A22 and the A264 to Tunbridge Wells, a delightful spot but noisy at week-ends.

Horsted Keynes, two miles to the south-west, is a gem of a village perched on a plateau where a web of lanes converge. Houses of many ages and shapes surround a green from which a steep lane dives down to a Norman church with a shingled spire and ancient cottages nearby. Beyond are lanes, lakes and woods. There is tranquillity here even on a bank holiday.

Clergymen have contributed very greatly through their diaries and notes to our knowledge of English social history. The Reverend Giles Moore, rector of Horsted Keynes from 1656 to 1680, kept a day book. His notes are matter-of-fact comments on matters of fact, day-to-day happenings, and their very unaffected simplicity brings to us the more vividly a picture of country life not so very long ago, yet long enough to have been almost forgotten by all except academic researchers.

"Never compound with any parishioner till you have first viewed their land, and seen what corne they have upon it that yeare and may have upon it ye next."

"I gave my wyfe 15/s. to lay out at S James Faire at Lindfield, all which shee spent except 2s. 6d. which shee never returned me."

"I received of my brother Brett, for a loade of hey and by

Clearing in the forest. Most of the woodlands along the Forest Ridge are managed; the trees are a crop. But paths wind their way through the trees.

him of mee the yeare before £1. It was worth at least 5/- more than he payd mee."

"I bargained with Edward Waters that hee should have 10s. in money for the trimming of mee by the yeare, I deducting 1s. 6d. for his tythes."

The lane down to Horsted Keynes passes a small hamlet set round a green, and a big house screened by a tall hedge. I knew the hamlet well as a boy and if anybody had told me that one day the name of it would ring round the world I would have stared at him in disbelief. The name of the

Birch Grove House, home of Mr Harold Macmillan. President John Kennedy met Mr Macmillan here in 1963.

hamlet is Birch Grove. The name of the house is Birch Grove House. Here, in 1963, Harold Macmillan, then British Prime Minister, met President Kennedy of the United States, and together they tried to open a road by which the world might find peace. Five months later John Kennedy was killed, victim of the assassin's bullet.

Two idyllic villages, Hartfield and Withyham, lie just north of the forest, where the heather and the bracken give way to rounded, grassy hills. Withyham is positively Arcadian with its meadows, green hills and lake with swans.

The whole district is served by East Grinstead, near the

Surrey border. This is a handsome and venerable town with a wide High Street, massive timber-framed walls, much Horsham slab roofing, and a commanding, pinnacled church tower completed in 1813. Its predecessor collapsed in 1785. East Grinstead is famous for the brilliant plastic surgery carried on at the Queen Victoria Hospital. It is also memorable for the peace of Sackville College, founded by the second Earl of Dorset as almshouses and completed in 1619. It is considered one of the finest Jacobean buildings in the country. Not that there is anything splendid about it; what you remember is the dignity and the quiet repose.

In the twelfth-century name, Grenestlda, we find again an echo of a forest clearing, a 'green place'. By about 1270 it had become Estgrenested to distinguish it from Westgrenested (West Grinstead), south of Horsham. Today East Grinstead is not only a good shopping centre but also a popular commuter town for London. Once you could also travel by rail from East Grinstead to Lewes; it was a single-line railway and when I travelled on it, which was often, I used to think of a parody somebody wrote of Wordsworth's poem:

> My heart leaps up when I behold
> A single railway line
> For then I know the wood and wold
> Are almost wholly mine.

Wood, wold and quietness are all there still, but, alas, the little railway fell a victim to 'economy' in 1955. A small stretch between Horsted Keynes and Sheffield Park survives through the enterprise of a private concern, the Bluebell Railway.

On the eastern edge of Ashdown Forest a Victorian and Edwardian creation, Crowborough, grew up. There are some eighteenth-century remnants, including the vicarage and the church tower. It is a pity so much sprawled over Beacon Hill, the highest point of the forest, 792 ft above sea level and higher than all but four of the Sussex downland hills. But time has mellowed the developers' profitable invasions, and modern Crowborough is proud of its wild setting and takes care of it.

The finest prospect of all the fine forest views is from nearby Camp Hill, whose crown of pines standing out against the sky is in itself dramatic. From Camp Hill the eastern Weald lies out before you like a carpet in manifold shades of blue, amber, green and silver-grey, with the enclosing downs in the far distance.

The South-East Forest Ridges

East and south-east of Ashdown Forest the scenery begins to change, subtly but none the less definitely. The view from Frant over Eridge Park is extensive and undoubtedly beautiful, yet there is a distinct difference. It is a more obviously

East Grinstead High Street. East Grinstead is well within the London commuter area, but the town also has a life and soul of its own, and it is graced by many ancient houses of heavy timber and plaster with Horsham slab roofs. Such views as this are by no means uncommon.

supervised countryside. Man is taking a more direct hand. You say good-bye to the heather, the deep forests and the open tracts of Ashdown, and you enter a land of small meadows, rounded hills, long ridges and deep valleys. Though many of these hills and ridge-tops are as high as the main forest ridge, and the prospect from them as wide and as satisfying, the feeling of wildness has gone. But not the remoteness, for it is off the main tourist beat. The countryside consists of small farms, chiefly dairy and stock rearing, interspersed with belts of woodland, including plantations of sweet chestnut. Hop gardens make an emphatic impact on the landscape around Burwash, Robertsbridge, Bodiam and Northiam, where oasthouses are accordingly plentiful, though as hops are now dried by electric power, many of the oasthouses have been converted into private houses, and some are used for storage. The broken countryside stretches right down the east side of the county, and comes to an abrupt halt in the cliffs of Hastings and the high ground at Winchelsea and above Rye.

Four large villages immediately to the east of Ashdown Forest always make an instant impression on the visitor. Each exudes a firm air of independence and self-sufficiency combined with the grace of an earlier age. The villages are Mayfield, Rotherfield, Wadhurst and Ticehurst, and they are all built on hilltops. All were important centres of the iron industry. The best way to approach Mayfield is from the south, from where you see it as a complete picture upon its rounded hill, with the short spire of St Dunstan's Church prominent on the crest. Coventry Patmore called it "the sweetest village in England". St Dunstan was born at Mayfield, was brought up at Glastonbury and was Archbishop of Canterbury from 960 to 988. He is said to have built a log church at Mayfield; a stone church which replaced it in the thirteenth century was almost entirely destroyed in 1389 by a fire, which also burnt down much of the village. Most of the present church was built in the fifteenth century.

In the fourteenth century a palace was built next to the church as a country house for the Archbishops of Canterbury. The last Archbishop to use it was Cranmer, who gave it to Henry VIII in 1545 in return for some Lancashire rectories. It then passed from hand to hand and eventually fell into decay, and was used as a quarry to the great benefit of Mayfield house builders. But in 1872 Cornelia Connelly, founder of the Society of the Holy Child, bought the ruins against everybody's advice, restored them and successfully incorporated them into a convent school.

Mayfield claims to have been the site where St Dunstan pinched the devil's nose with tongs; but so also does Glastonbury.

Rotherfield is a spacious, friendly village on top of a 500-ft hill. The Saxons had a settlement there, and Berhtwald, Duke of the South Saxons, built a church on the highest point in 792. He explains in his will why he did so. He "fell into a sickness of which none of the doctors was able to heal me; but I heard that in Gaul, at a monastery of the holy martyrs Dionysious, Rusticus and Eleutherious, many miracles had happened through these saints." So Berhtwald made a pilgrimage to France, got better and as a thanksgiving "built a church on my estate in the property called Redrefeld". It was dedicated to St Denys (Dionysious) and its successor, built in the thirteenth century, retained the dedication.

Rotherfield has produced the most extraordinary legend I have ever heard. Its women were said to have been equipped with two ribs more than Rotherfield men, which accounted for their unusual height. Nobody knows why they were invested with such superiority but they certainly needed extra strength if they had to carry water to the village from the surrounding streams. The climb is very stiff.

The eastern River Rother (not to be confused with the western Rother at the other end of the county) rises about a mile south of the village. The source of the Medway and one of the sources of the Ouse are in the same district.

Wadhurst is a large village with something of the atmosphere of a town, which, in fact, it can rightfully claim to be

St Dunstan's Church, Mayfield. The lower part of the tower is what remains of the original built in the twelfth century. The rest is a rebuilding after a disastrous fire in 1389. The church stands on the crest of a hill and is a landmark for many miles.

Brede Levels landscape. A medley of small meadows, woodland and hop gardens, extending away to a hazy distance. The photograph was taken at Brede.

under a charter granted by Henry III in 1233. It is a busy place, yet there is about it a mellowness often to be found in places which have lost their *raison d'etre* but have not thereby decayed. The floor of the church bears witness to the importance of Wadhurst in the iron-smelting business. It includes thirty fine cast-iron grave slabs. Their dates span 182 years, from 1617 to 1799.

Ticehurst also has the character of a small town, but, again like Wadhurst, a certain sense of dignity. Ticehurst is an excellent example of how harmony can spring from great variety. White weather boarding mingles with red tiles; walls of hanging tiles mingle with walls of conventional brick and walls with black oak timber framing. And not a discordant note. The church dates almost wholly from the fourteenth century, and it is all of a piece – warm, amber sandstone that glows in the sun.

All four villages overlook the Rother Valley. From Mayfield, which stands on the brink, it seems almost a ravine, and the ridge the other side is succeeded by further ridges which gradually disappear in a blue haze. Once over there, unless you keep to the A265, travel becomes a matter of twists and turns and ups and downs, and none the worse for that, though E. V. Lucas suffered a fit of the grumps on account of "... this switch back district ... where one eminence is painfully won only to reveal another."

The natural starting point for the country south of the Rother is Heathfield. But what is Heathfield? Or, rather,

Wadhurst, once one of the most important centres of the Wealden iron industry.

where and which is Heathfield? There is a long stretch of shops along the main road, but one feels at once that this cannot be all, and, indeed, it is not. The original Heathfield, now called Old Heathfield, is built on the lip of a valley about a mile and a half from the street, a prominent church with a tall shingled spire, a snug inn and pretty cottages clustered round.

The church was heavily 'restored' in the nineteenth century but a good deal of the original thirteenth-century work remains. There was rebuilding in 1380 after fire damage, and this was the origin of the inn, the *Star.* It was built to provide shelter and sustenance for the men working on the church.

There are several other independent groups of cottages, all part of Heathfield and all built round Heathfield Park, home of General George Augustus Eliott, successful defender of Gibraltar in the French-Spanish siege of 1779-83. He was created Baron Heathfield of Gibraltar in 1887.

One of these 'little Heathfields', Cade Street, commemorates another famous man, the rebel Jack Cade. It is said that Cade was caught about here in 1450 by Alexander Iden, Sheriff of Kent. Shakespeare, placing the scene in Kent, describes it in the second part of Henry VI (Act IV, Scene x). But Cade Street does not really derive from the rebel's name, for at least a hundred years before Cade was born the place was called Kattestrete, cart street. Still, the appropriate spot is marked by 'Jack Cade's stone'.

Six miles away, in 1902, Kipling found 'the Very-Own House', which is Bateman's, Burwash, understandably one of the most frequently visited houses owned by the National Trust. Kipling was then thirty-six, and he lived at Bateman's until his death in 1936. It is a big sandstone house built in 1634 for an iron master, and is a measure of the prosperity which the iron industry brought to the Weald. So far as possible, Bateman's is maintained as Kipling left it. His study is kept so exactly as it was when he worked in it that you feel almost an intruder as you go in. A wooded hill beyond the garden is the Pook's Hill of *Puck of Pook's Hill,* written in 1906. It is not the original name of the hill but today nobody ever calls it anything else.

Bateman's, Burwash, home of Rudyard Kipling from 1902 until his death in 1936. The house was built in 1634 for an iron master and it is now owned by the National Trust.

To travel from Burwash to Brightling to Battle entails a delicious meandering along the criss-cross lanes which so exhausted poor Lucas. You will be lucky if you do not lose yourself, but what of it? There will be woodmen cutting, farm men haying or somebody looking over the cows, and they will not only tell you the way but talk to you, so that your getting lost may earn you a considerable bonus.

From every hilltop you are guided by a conspicuous landmark, a tall obelisk jutting up to the sky. This would be most convenient if you were wafting through the air, but the lanes do not waft. They wiggle, and when several gather together in a valley you quickly lose your sense of direction. However, when eventually you reach the obelisk you are rewarded, provided the weather is clear, by an extraordinary view. You are on top of Brightling Down (nothing to do with

(Right) *The obelisk on the top of Brightling Down – this has nothing to do with the range of Sussex Downs, which are about 13 miles south-west. The obelisk, called the Brightling Needle, is one of 'mad' Jack Fuller's follies.*

(Below) *Kipling's study at Bateman's, Burwash, which he called his workshop. It is maintained exactly as the poet left it. The blocks on the chair legs were put there to his measurements, so that he could sit at just the right height at his desk. Kipling was a small man.*

the chalk downs), 646 ft high, the highest point of the southern ridges, and your eye ranges in a wide circumference over the ridges and dips to Ashdown Forest, into Kent and across to the downs. The prospect to the downs is particularly interesting, for from this viewpoint, well east of their beginning, you can see clearly the diagonal line they form across the county.

This is Fuller country. They called him mad Jack Fuller and he was famous in his day. He came of a wealthy iron-founding family. His evils were very evil and his good was very good. He had extensive slave interests. He found work for local people. He bought Bodiam Castle to prevent its demolition. He was Member of Parliament for Lewes from 1801 to 1812 and once called the Speaker "an insignificant little fellow in a wig". For that he was carried out of the House.

Fuller, who lived at Rose Hill (now called Brightling Park), firmly stamped his personality on the district by putting up a number of follies, of which one is the obelisk, called the Brightling Needle. The most macabre was his own tomb, a pyramid in the churchyard. He built it twenty-four years before his death. Pitt offered him a peerage, which he refused, declaring, "I was born Jack Fuller and Jack Fuller I'll die", which he did in 1834 aged seventy-seven and a bachelor, and was duly interred in his pyramid.

Brightling village stands in a sort of recess in the side of a hill, a happy mingling of red roofs, sandstone walls and big trees clustered round a large church. The church was originally built about 1066, and has been altered and enlarged considerably through the centuries. You could easily pass by and miss it, as you could miss so many small villages in this pleasant hinterland.

Battle is the child of the abbey, which, as we all know, is the child of the battle. William, having won, founded the abbey, thus, it is said, fulfilling a vow made before the battle began, and the altar stands where Harold fell. Compared with today's vastly more complicated wars, this little fight on October 14, 1066, might seem scarcely worth mentioning. Yet it changed our history in a way that nothing else has ever done, both social and political.

Jack Fuller's mausoleum, a pyramid in Brightling churchyard. He built it in 1810.

The abbey developed and grew through the years. The great gatehouse, one of the finest in England, was built in 1338 by Abbot Alan de Ketling. Henry VIII destroyed what William began. The abbey was one of the wealthiest in the land at its dissolution in 1538, when the king granted it to Sir Anthony Browne, who dismantled it with diabolical efficiency.

The town bestrides a long ridge. It is the successor of the rough living quarters constructed by the workmen who were building the abbey. Nothing remains of these early habitations, which were gradually replaced by more substantial buildings. Some of the houses, or parts of them, have

(Above) The great gatehouse of Battle Abbey. It was built in 1338 and survived the Dissolution. It stands dramatically at the top of the town, and first-time visitors think it is a castle. Battle Abbey was, in fact, fortified against possible atack by the French.

(Right) The long street of Battle stretches down from the great gatehouse. The simple timber dwellings of the men who built the Abbey stood where the present buildings now stand.

descended from the abbey in a more literal sense. It is no coincidence that the stones of their walls have the same warm amber tinge as the abbey; they came from the abbey kitchen, which was pulled down in 1687 and sold at four shillings a load.

The gatehouse overshadows a heavily timber-framed house called the Pilgrim's Rest, probably built about 1420, perhaps

BANK

replacing an earlier building. As its name suggests, it was a rest house for pilgrims visiting the abbey.

Battle was a Benedictine abbey. Five miles north, in 1176, the Cistercians also founded an abbey, Robertsbridge. They cleared and cultivated a particularly obstinate tract of the Weald, and today the ruins of this abbey are incorporated in Abbey Farm.

Robertsbridge has a more modern claim to fame: the manufacture of cricket bats, which are made by craftsmen in workshops half-hidden among woods on a ridge above the village. Robertsbridge bats are used by world-renowned players, but the enterprise started almost by accident and practically in self-defence. A local cricket enthusiast, Mr L. J. Nicolls, started making bats for himself and his friends about 1870. These bats created such a demand that Mr Nicolls was obliged either to say no or to set up commercially. He set up commercially. The great Dr W. G. Grace used a Nicolls bat; it was with a Nicolls bat that he knocked up his hundredth century and with the same bat scored a thousand runs in one month of May.

The countryside undergoes a marked change east of Battle and Robertsbridge. The Wealden ridges are pierced by long and wide inlets thrusting in from what the local people call comprehensively the Marsh, the heart of which is Romney Marsh. The Rivers Rother, Tillingham and Brede make their placid way through extensive levels which were once covered by the sea and are now cropped by sheep. These marsh pastures are cut about by innumerable rivulets, dykes, ditches and channels, where the wildfowl gather in winter and where the redshank pipes his plaintive cry all the year round. Above the levels the land remains as undulating as ever, and on the slopes the hop gardens are often extensive, especially round Bodiam.

Bodiam, however, is better known for its castle than for its hops. It makes the perfect picture, set four-square in its moat, with a massive round tower at each corner and white

Craftsmen at work in the Robertsbridge cricket bat workshop. Top cricketers use bats made here.

Bodiam Castle, built in 1385 as a possible defence against the French, who could easily have stormed up the Rother estuary. It is said to be one of the best-preserved examples of medieval military architecture, though the interior was dismantled by Cromwell. The French did not come. The castle is now owned by the National Trust.

In the summer the car park at Bodiam Castle is usually full, but the lanes leading to the village are quiet and shady.

water lilies to set off the grey stone. It was built by Sir Edward Dalyngrigge in 1385 as part of a possible second-line defence against the French, who frequently sacked the coastal towns, particularly Rye and Winchelsea less than 10 miles off. The Rother was then navigable as far as Bodiam. But the French never came. It seems the nearest Bodiam ever got to action was in 1483, during the Wars of the Roses, when the Whites took it from the Reds, and then, apparently, without a struggle. Nevertheless, Cromwell 'slighted' the castle, despite its non-belligerent life, and the interior was dismantled. Then it steadily deteriorated until Jack Fuller saved it. Lord Curzon bought it in 1917, thoroughly repaired the exterior, and left it to the National Trust on his death in 1926.

Ewhurst, across the valley from Bodiam, provides a reminder that Cobbett was not the only tireless rider over England. Another was John Wesley. In many respects the two men were similar. Both were stirred to indignation by poverty and injustice and both trenchantly laid about them with voice and pen. Wesley, riding through East Sussex, stayed at Ewhurst at the invitation of the Anglican curate there, the Reverend John Richardson, who became a great friend and follower of Wesley. The preacher slept in a heavily timbered, sixteenth-century house with a superb view over the Rother Valley, and I have often wondered what thoughts crossed his mind on a sunny morning as he gazed over the bright meadows before breakfast. The house is still called the Preacher's House.

I cannot think of a village in this eastern corner of Sussex where one would not wish to linger. They have not set out to achieve attractiveness: they do not have to. It is enough that the villages are themselves. They are quiet, tidy, unassuming and small, with Northiam the exception in size. Northiam is a big village, but what strikes you most forcibly is not its extent but its whiteness. It is a village of white weather-boards, and one of these weather-boarded houses, built just before the nineteenth century, is the biggest of its kind in Sussex and probably anywhere in the country. It is prominent at a corner of the green, where, under an oak in 1573, Queen Elizabeth I was given lunch.

Immaculate Sedlescombe lies on either side of the Hawkhurst-Hastings road, with well house and pump in the middle of the green.

Iden, on a plateau above the Rother Levels, looks like a corner of Normandy, complete with pigs in old apple orchards. The pride of Brede, overlooking the Brede Levels, is Brede Place, where Sir Winston Churchill often stayed, and where the sculptress Clare Sheridan lived and worked for some years. Brede Place is no mansion; it is small, warm and friendly, built in 1350 by a knight of Edward III and considerably enlarged in about 1570.

The sixteenth-century house at Ewhurst in which John Wesley sometimes stayed. It is still called the Preacher's House.

Oasthouses are now desirable residences. Eastern and south-eastern Sussex are hop-growing areas, but as hops are now dried by electricity, many oasthouses have been converted into private dwellings, like these at Ewhurst.

A short distance on, Rye and Winchelsea gaze at one another across the level marsh.

The Low Plain

The Low Plain extends north-west across the county from the coast between Eastbourne and Bexhill, where the marshes of the Pevensey Levels reach down to the sea. It is nearly all clay, with occasional stretches of alluvium and sand. In many places it is not much higher than sea level, and this is why the downs, rising abruptly from the low land, seem so much higher, viewed from the plain, than they actually are. It is heavy land, and difficult to cultivate. Farmers always do their utmost to drill all their corn in the autumn. If they leave any for the spring it may never be sown, for it may be impossible to break down the wet clods. It holds the frost and fog in winter and it parches and cracks quickly in drought, when the heat strikes up into your face from the hot earth.

Yet though the land is low, it is not flat; it is gently undulating and does not lack interest. Occasional wet patches and pools, mute echoes of boggiest Andredsweald, defy the most determined attempts at land-drainage. Rivers and streams flow slowly, having come down from the forest ridges, executing wide loops as they follow the gradually descending land. Stupendous oaks flourish on the clay and occasionally you may find a belt of woodland which seems to show evidence of natural regeneration over a long period. Such a wood is unlikely to be wholly a descendant of Andredsweald, but in part it may well be so. The Sussex Trust for Nature Conservation owns and carefully preserves a woodland belt of this kind called The Mens, near Wisborough Green. These woods, covering 360 acres, may have partially regenerated after the iron furnaces closed. They give us a glimpse of the old low Weald, just as the Wakehurst woods give us some idea of the nature of the old ridge forests.

At the beginning of the plain, the rooftops of Pevensey village and the rugged remains of the Roman-Norman castle rise sharply above the flat meadows in a series of silhouettes. Sheep and cattle graze the meadows, children play within the fortress walls, men and women enjoy a quiet drink at an inn.

(Above) Pevensey High Street from the east gate of the castle. The Old Mint House is on the left.

(Right) Roman bastion protecting the east gate of Pevensey Castle. The herringbone brickwork at the top is eleventh-century repairs.

It is hard to realize that this place, leisurely and peaceful despite much traffic, has behind it a history of drama and violence. Indeed, the very name of Pevensey seems to echo like a clarion call.

Pevensey owes its origin to its strategic position, a shallow hill at the end of a lonely promontory. The Romans called it Anderida and built a massive fort on it, one of ten (or

Inner facing of Roman wall at Pevensey Castle. The Romans made a great deal of use of rectangular stone blocks bonded together with iron-hard mortar. The Roman work in this fort, which enclosed ten acres, has lasted better than the Norman keep at the eastern end.

possibly eleven) placed at key positions round the coast from Brancaster in Norfolk to Porchester in Hampshire, 'the Saxon Shore'. The waters of an estuary lapped the walls of the fort, which was thus provided with an excellent harbour. Inland stretched a wilderness of marsh and dank impenetrable forest, the unexplored Silva Anderida.

The forts were built to repel invaders, assumed until recently to have been the Saxons. There is now some doubt about this. The fort of Anderida, built towards the end of the third century or early in the fourth, had walls twelve feet thick and often twenty feet high. It enclosed about ten acres. Bastions projected from the walls, which could thereby be covered at all points by cross-fire. There were only two entrances, one to the west and landward, the other to the east, giving on to the estuary. The Saxons of that time had nothing like the strength or skill necessary to subdue defences of such magnitude, and it has been suggested that the forts might have been built by the brilliant mariner-rebel, Carausius, not against Saxons but against his fellow-Romans.

Be that as it may, the forts were certainly used eventually against increasingly formidable bands of Saxon raiders. As Rome weakened, the legions were withdrawn from Britain, and Anderida, like the rest of the province, lay defenceless. Then the raiders came in hordes, and in 491. according to the *Anglo-Saxon Chronicle*, they massacred all the Britons of Anderida to a man. Obscurity fell upon Anderida, which became known as Peueneséa (possibly Pefen's river). It did not appear again in the pattern of English history until September 28, 1066, when Norman William arrived with a fleet of nearly seven hundred ships and ten thousand men.

William gave Pevensey to his half-brother, Robert of Mortmain, who, like any Norman, knew first-class defence work when he saw it. He repaired the fort, still in good shape after nearly six centuries. He also founded a borough, and Pevensey became a port of considerable consequence. It was accorded the privilege of its own mint, mentioned in Domesday Book. In the early thirteenth century it also became a 'limb' of the Cinque Port of Hastings, and its borough seal is the oldest in the possession of any of these historic ports.

It also became a place of intrigue and strife, and the turbulence was eventually stopped not by men at arms but by nature: the sea silted up and left Pevensey stranded. As the town's importance depended entirely on its maritime life, it presently ceased to have any importance at all, but it retained its borough status until 1883.

A busy road runs through Pevensey today, and many visitors flock to see the castle. Yet the place out of season is quiet enough. It is a smallish village now and a mile of marsh pasture separates it from the sea. A large building near the castle, called the Old Mint House, is claimed to stand on the site of the original minthouse. It dates from about 1432 but was much altered in the sixteenth century; it was occupied by the sixteenth-century physician and wit, Andrew Borde

(Merry Andrew). A little square building nearby wears a faintly Spanish air but is actually the Old Court House and Town Hall, probably the smallest example of either in England.

There are no large and only two middle-sized towns on the low plain. These two are Haywards Heath and Burgess Hill, places which have grown up with the railway and have now become the hub of mid-Sussex. There is, however, a fair number of small towns and very large villages, and it is frequently hard to decide whether a place is town or village. Their origins are firmly rooted in their own countryside and their histories are long.

The first of these little towns, sitting just above the web of brooks, rivulets and dykes which criss-cross Pevensey Levels, is Hailsham, a prosperous market town with a large, much-restored, fifteenth-century church. The bells of this church were cast close by, and until comparatively recently rang the curfew each evening.

Herstmonceux, also just above the levels, is the home of a flourishing rural industry, born about the middle of the last century, when a certain Mr Thomas Smith decided that the heavy and cumbersome receptacle then in use for all pick-and-carry jobs on farm and garden, and little changed since Anglo-Saxon days, should give way to something better. He therefore invented the Sussex trug, with which every gardener all over the country is familiar. It was a light but strong boat-shaped basket made of willow slats firmly nailed to a light chestnut frame, one part of which formed the handle. It gained a prize medal and a diploma of merit at the great Hyde Park exhibition of 1851, where it also caught the eye of Queen Victoria, who ordered a number to be specially made for herself.

Thomas Smith would have made a great hit in our modern advertising age. In 1851 there were other means of transport than walking, but not for Thomas Smith in such august circumstances. He walked the sixty miles from Herstmonceux to London and delivered his royal order at Buckingham Palace personally. The trugs are still made entirely by hand at the Herstmonceux workshop, and the basic pattern remains the same.

In the trug-makers' workshop at Herstmonceux. These light but strong wooden baskets are familiar in gardens throughout England, and considerable numbers are also exported, particularly to the United States.

Michelham Priory, built in 1229 for Augustan canons, partially destroyed after the Dissolution of 1536, converted into a private Tudor dwelling, and now in the safe-keeping of the Sussex Archaeological Trust.

Herstmonceux is also the home of the Royal Greenwich Observatory, for which the Admiralty bought Herstmonceux Castle in 1946. Like Bodiam, this castle stands picturesquely in a moat. Its main claim to distinction is that it was one of the first large buildings in Britain to be constructed of brick. It was built in 1440, dismantled in 1777, and restored in 1913; another and thorough restoration job followed in 1933. It is a fine sight, with its battlements and turrets, but it was designed to be lived in rather than fought from.

About two miles west of Hailsham, one of the greatest treasures of Sussex, Michelham Priory, stands upon a six-acre island surrounded by a seven-acre moat. The Priory was built in 1229 for Augustan canons, and the beautiful stone building has survived many vicissitudes in its chequered history, particularly since the Dissolution of 1536, when it was partially destroyed. It entered the safe-keeping of the Sussex Archaeological Trust in 1959. The approach to the house is through a sixty-foot gateway tower, and a great barn borders the moat with beams so immense that you can scarcely take your eyes off them.

Horam (Horeham Road until comparatively recently) is a pioneer area of the quickly reviving English wine-growing enterprises. It is about five miles north of Hailsham; and on the way you pass Hellingly, where the churchyard is circular and probably of Saxon origin.

Uckfield, almost on the forest ridge, suffers from its situation just below the convergence of two main roads to Eastbourne. In one long street shops, offices and houses stand cheek-by-jowl in an astonishing medley of style, age and size. Yet there are not many discordant notes, and off that evil road there are some quiet corners, like Monk's Walk, which suggests that pilgrims went this way to Canterbury. So does Puddingcake Lane – pilgrims paid their coppers through a small window and were given pudding and cake.

Commons and village greens are a major feature of the plain. Some are beautiful, like Ringmer, Lindfield, Henfield and Wisborough Green. Some have become overgrown. One, the 400-acre Chailey Common, has been rescued through the intelligent co-operation of naturalists and local authorities, and is now a local nature reserve.

A perusal of village histories very quickly and completely dispels the notion that demonstrations are a modern phenomenon. The greens were frequently the scene of lusty gatherings, and Ringmer provides an epic example. The thirties and forties of the nineteenth century were times of great distress for the village labourers. In 1830 a band of a hundred and fifty farm workers met Lord Gage on Ringmer green and gave him a petition requesting that their wages be raised from 9d to 2s 6d a day; they also wanted the dismissal of the Poor Law overseers, renowned for cruelty, and particularly the Ringmer overseer, who was described as "lost to all feelings of humanity". Lord Gage went away for a while, thought about it, and agreed, whereon, said *The Times,* the men dispersed with hymns and tears of joy. But, since they were men of mettle, they broke up the village grindstone on their way home.

The Reverend Gilbert White often stayed at Ringmer with his aunt, Mrs Rebecca Snooke. There he met Timothy, the tortoise, who lived in Mrs Snooke's garden for forty-six years. Timothy became familiar to naturalists through White's notes about him in *The Natural History of Selborne.* White took him to Selborne when Mrs Snooke died in 1780; his carapace is preserved in London's Natural History Museum.

Two Englishmen who helped build America chose Ringmer brides. William Penn, the Quaker founder of Pennsylvania, married Gulielma Springett, daughter of Sir William Springett, of Broyle Place; and John Harvard, founder of the university, married Ann Sadler, daughter of a Ringmer vicar. The two women join company with Timothy on the village sign, which was unveiled by the American ambassador in 1923.

Cuckfield, like Uckfield, is nearly on the forest ridge. It was once a small market town, and its urban traditions reach back to 1254, when it was granted a charter. Cuckfield did not want the railway, and Haywards Heath, where the railway went, eventually became the bigger town. The two have now practically joined up, but Cuckfield still retains the lively atmosphere of a self-contained little town. Henry Kingsley, novelist brother of Charles, lived here in a heavily beamed, seventeenth-century house that used to be called Attrees. Today it is called Kingsleys.

Lindfield is also more or less joined to Haywards Heath, but nevertheless remains a village with many charms. Apart

Chailey Common was rescued from total obliteration by scrub and is now a local nature reserve. There are about 14,000 acres of common land in Sussex and most of them have scrub problems since there are now few commoners to cut and graze the land.

from the gracious green, there is a half-mile long main street, an architectural historian's paradise. It includes at least thirty ancient buildings, some medieval.

Henfield is more town than village, but it contains much mellowed and pleasant architecture. The minute you step off the busy High Street you find yourself in an altogether quieter, more retiring world of lanes and pedestrian ways, with a good deal of timbered and plastered houses. Henfield is a pioneer of cricket, for its club was founded in 1771. Henfield also pioneered something a great deal less pleasant – the plague. It broke out here fifty-six years before the great epidemic of London. About sixty people died between September 13, 1609, and January 16 the following year.

Steyning was once a thriving Saxon port at the head of a wide estuary which pierced far inland through the Adur gap. It was a royal possession in King Alfred's day, and the king's father, Aethelwulf, may have been buried there in 858, though he is also said to have been buried at Chichester. Harbour and estuary silted up in the fourteenth century, and Steyning, like Pevensey, was left high and dry, but it did not fade away as a consequence. Steyning turned its face the other way, to the land, and became an important market town.

The church is only part of a much larger Norman building. It stands on the site of a Saxon church founded by St Cuthman in the eighth century. Edward the Confessor gave it to the Benedictine Abbey of Fécamp in 1047, and the monks established a collegiate church. The surviving twelfth-century interior is considered to be among the finest late Norman architecture in the country.

Steyning lies to the west of the River Adur and north of the downs. The twin villages, Bramber and Upper Beeding, straddle the river at the northern end of the Adur gap, where the downs fall sharply away, leaving the villages on the plain. It is a position of great strategic importance and the Norman, William de Braose, lost no time in fortifying it with a castle on a mound. Cromwell's men ripped it apart in 1641; a few gaunt ruins still rear up dramatically against the sky.

Storrington, Pulborough and Billingshurst, towards the western end of the plain, are all busy villages on main roads.

Seventeenth-century houses in Church Street, Steyning. The building on the right is dated 1611.

*(*Above*) The Old House, Pulborough, partly fifteenth and partly sixteenth century, is shored up on top of a bank beside the road that used to be Stane Street. Its extraordinary situation makes it a popular subject for amateur photographers. It has smuggling associations.*

*(*Left*) This is a popular pausing place for motorists on the A283 Brighton to Petworth road. The lake at Storrington.*

There are quiet ways running off Storrington's main street, and when you go into Brewer's Yard, with its 400-year-old brewery buildings converted into cottages, you wonder where the twentieth century has gone. Francis Thompson, the poet, lived at Storrington from 1888 to 1893.

Parham, about two miles from Storrington, must be one of the most exquisitely sited houses in the country, crowning a ridge with a wide view over a timbered park to the downs. It is also one of the loveliest of the Sussex Elizabethan mansions, perhaps sharing the honour with Danny, near Hurstpierpoint, and Wiston, under Chanctonbury. It was begun in 1577 by Sir Thomas Palmer, who sailed with Drake to Cadiz.

Stane Street, overlaid with tarmac, runs straight through Billingshurst and Pulborough. It is possible that a varied Roman-British community grew up in the Pulborough area, centred on Stane Street. It is certain that an important posting station was established at Hardham, the first out of Noviomagus on the way to Londinium. Transport along the main Roman roads was quick, and it was not equalled, let alone surpassed, until the stage coach era of the nineteenth century. The posting stations would include inns and stables, and no doubt houses for civilians who worked there, and those residents would need shops. The theory of a mixed Roman community, perhaps partly civilian and partly military, is supported by the discovery of two villas. It is an arresting idea, an oasis of civilization in the middle of the great wild, but how tantalizing that we should know so little of the details which made up the Roman administration in this country. What, for instance, was the Hardham posting station called? Or Stane Street?

Hardham has another claim on our notice today. The walls of its little church are covered with murals unique in England because of their early date (about 1100) and their completeness. At some date unknown, perhaps in the thirteenth century, they were entirely covered with plaster and remained hidden until 1866. Like the paintings at Clayton, the

The upper Arun Valley, where the river runs slowly beside flat water meadows. A view near Pulborough.

Hardham murals were intended to be taken literally. They include nativity scenes, Christ among the doctors, Adam and Eve, St George in action against the Saracens and four pictures demonstrating the fate of those who sin too much.

A labyrinth of narrow lanes intersects this part of the low Weald. One of them winds along to Shipley, another to the *Blue Idol.* Since the purpose of the Shipley lane is simply to get you there and not to speed you on somewhere else, you can walk about the village without fear of sudden death from rushing vehicles. Agriculture pursues its vital, unhurried course, the infant Adur wanders through a level meadow and the shadows from the sails of the mill that Belloc bought move slowly over the grass as the hours pass. You soon come to feel that haste is not only unnecessary but unseemly, and not only here but elsewhere also.

It was John Ireland's great delight in his latter years to sit in the churchyard and watch the view across the meadow, with the little Adur and an ancient farmhouse the other side. The composer lived at Washington about six miles away, but at his own wish he was buried at Shipley. He died in 1962 when he was 83.

Belloc lived at Shipley from 1906 until he died in 1953 in a big rambling house called King's Land, which he bought with some surrounding land on which the windmill stood. The mill has been restored to working condition and is maintained in Belloc's memory.

The church contains a famous thirteenth-century enamelled reliquary from Limoges. the chief European centre for enamellers from the twelfth to the fourteenth century. The Shipley reliquary is said to be one of the most beautiful specimens in existence. It was on loan to the Victoria and Albert Museum from 1917 to 1939. Now it occupies a niche in the church wall.

The *Blue Idol* is closely connected with worship, but of a kind far removed from idols. It is a Quaker meeting house and guest house, and William Penn worshipped there. Penn

The view John Ireland loved. This photograph was taken from Shipley churchyard, near the composer's grave.

The Blue Idol. This beautiful old house dates, at least in part, from about 1580. Members of the Society of Friends (the Quakers) faced persecution for worshipping in their chosen way at this house.

William Penn spoke to fellow Quakers in this room. The meeting house in the Blue Idol, near Billingshurst.

lived at Warminghurst, four miles away, for fifteen years, and he regularly rode over for worship at the *Blue Idol* then a farmhouse called Little Slatters, home of a Friend named John Shaw. At Mr Shaw's invitation, the Quakers converted one end of Little Slatters into a meeting house. This is a cheerful but dignified little room, full of light despite massive

*(*Above*) Fletching parish church. Simon de Montfort's army encamped at Fletching in 1264 on the eve of the Battle of Lewes fought on the downs about eight miles away. The night before the battle, de Montfort and his knights prayed in the church, and it is said that a number of these knights, slain in the batle, were brought back to Fletching and buried under the nave in full armour. Edward Gibbon, author of* Decline and Fall of the Roman Empire, *is also buried in this church.*

*(*Left*) Amberley Wild Brooks, probably derived from 'Weald' brooks. This is an extensive area of marsh and water meadows of great interest to the naturalist. It is rich in both bird and plant life.*

(Above) *Sheffield Park Gardens, where the forest ridge begins to give way to the low plain of the Weald. The gardens, now owned by the National Trust, cover 142 acres, which include 62 acres of woodland and parkland. They were laid out on different levels in the eighteenth century, but given their present form in the twentieth. They are noted for their brilliant spring and autumn displays, and also for rare specimen conifers, golden larch, eucalyptus and gentians.*

(Right) *This stark relic is all that remains of the once powerful Bramber Castle. Cromwell's men demolished it.*

black timbers, unexpectedly high because the Friends took out the first floor, except at one end where it was converted into a gallery.

Nobody knows exactly when the house was built. Probably the oldest part to be seen today was constructed in about 1580. It is a long, lovely place, sturdy timber-framed walls supporting an immaculate roof of Horsham slabs. And nobody knows for certain how the building came by its extraordinary name. It may have happened between 1793 and 1869 when the meeting house was closed and colour-washed in blue —and became, therefore, the idle blue meeting house?

One could spend whole days happily wandering about these lanes, now and then discovering a little village, all with a hearty Saxon smack about their names, like Warninglid, Slaugham and West Chiltington; West Grinstead, Thakeham and Nuthurst; Barns Green, Dragons Green and Staplefield.

The countryside changes quickly the other side of the fifteenth-century Stopham bridge, west of Pulborough, and it is soon clear that this is no longer low Weald. Fittleworth, partly on the hillside and partly on the banks of the Rother, marks a kind of boundary. Beyond are deep valleys and rounded hills, leading up to Petworth, the heaths and the pine woods. We are back in the north-west.

Typical river countryside of the low Weald. The photograph was taken near the junction of the Arun and the Rother.

The harbour at Littlehampton at the mouth of the Arun is occupied by commercial, fishing and pleasure craft.

CHAPTER FOUR

THE COASTAL TOWNS

Nearly all the Sussex coastal towns are holiday resorts, and they owe their development as such to the 'seaside fever' of the late eighteenth and nineteenth centuries. They are in Sussex but most are not entirely of Sussex, though nearly all have sprung from typical Sussex farming or fishing villages.

Now they have grown too large. They run into one another. Except for a few small breaks, one single belt of bricks and mortar reaches solidly along the coastline from Bognor Regis to Newhaven, a distance of over thirty miles. Even in the little gaps, the pressure of the houses can be felt. It is difficult and often impossible to tell when you are out of one town and in another.

Yet, paradoxically, every one of these towns has in recent years developed a strong sense of independence and social awareness. Cultural and amenity societies have sprung up; local history, archaeology and nature conservation are all closely studied. Museums have shaken off their tradition of dust and fusty language and are brightly laid out and labelled in words everybody can understand. While these movements have not generally developed from the roots of Sussex, they have greatly helped to foster an understanding not only of their own localities but of the county as a whole.

Unlike most of the coastal holiday towns, Bognor Regis was preconceived. It was deliberately planned as a seaside resort by Sir Richard Hotham, a Southwark hatter, in the 1790s. It was designed especially for the refined and the genteel, and might have been called Hothampton. Sir Richard died before his dream town was completed but not before he had built himself a big house in a big park, now called Hotham Park. The 'Regis' came in 1929 after King George V had spent a convalescence at Aldwick. Only since the last war has Bognor been given a definite focal point in a big new development by the pier. And the twentieth century has produced a successor to Sir Richard as holiday planner: Bognor has a Butlin's Holiday Camp, designed by Sir Billy himself.

Bognor is blessed by miles of sand on which children can safely play and horses can be given early morning gallops. Queen Victoria thought of it with affection and called it 'dear little Bognor'. One feels that the town does not wish to lose this image entirely.

Littlehampton, too, has sand and also space. People whose knowledge of the town is limited to their efforts to get through it will greet such a remark with derision. It is true, however, and it gives this town an advantage over may other resorts. Congested the town most certainly is, but the space is on the front, and traffic cannot get at you when you are there.

For this boon of space and safety you have to thank three things in particular, the green, the sands and the dunes. The green lies between town and sea, a long, wide stretch of grass, a bit like the Hove lawns but more informal. The green gives way to the sands – and what sands! When the tide is out you can almost forget the sea. The other space factor, the dunes, are part of that two-mile coastal stretch to which I have referred in Chapter One on the coastal plain. They extend westward from the banks of the Arun, which here flows swiftly into the sea with the green on one side and the dunes on the other. They are a tumbled mixture of sand hillocks and rough grass, which film-makers have been quick to appreciate when they have needed to simulate a desert.

Littlehampton is both a port and a resort. As a holiday town, it is entirely a nineteenth-century development. At the end of the eighteenth century its population was about 600. Artists and writers were the pioneers of what was to come, preceding the annual family seaside holiday which became such a strong Littlehampton tradition.

Littlehampton's origin takes us back a long way. There was a Roman-British settlement where the town now stands, or thereabouts. The Normans realized its value as a port, and after the Conquest much shipping, commercial and otherwise, plied to and from Normandy. William Rufus sailed into the port in 1097. His niece, Matilda, is said to have landed there in 1139 to dispute the Crown with Stephen. Prisoners from Crecy were brought into Littlehampton. About forty years later, eighty French vessels captured in the Channel were also taken there: they were carrying 20,000 tons of wine.

The mouth of the Arun, once a wide estuary, gradually silted up and marsh pasture took over, but Littlehampton refused to choke. A cut was made in 1626 and another, the present outlet, in the 1730s. And the little port never closed; it is still active, and so are its shipyards, which build lifeboats for the Royal National Lifeboat Institution. Sailing and powered craft mingle with fishing vessels towards the river mouth and swans weave their way among them all.

This maritime part of the town is a busy, bustling area. The smells of tar and timber blend with the sharp tang that blows up from the sea. Old flint cottages line little streets and alleyways, and the cottage groups are relieved here and there by the gay sign of a pub.

Worthing, the biggest of the coastal towns after Brighton, occupies one of the warmest spots in the country, perhaps actually the warmest. For many years, therefore, people have gone to live there permanently, so that now the town is full of what estate agents call 'much sought-after' residential areas. They seem to stretch for miles, pleasant houses in pleasant gardens beside pleasant tree-lined roads. Villages have been swallowed, and (more serious) so have extensive market gardens. Worthing's horticultural produce is early and plentiful, because of the combination of the warm climate and a highly fertile soil. The excellence and bounty of the Worthing market gardens is not excelled anywhere in the coastal plain, or, for that matter, anywhere in England. What is left of them should not be sterilized by 'desirable residences'.

Worthing is not the fuddy-duddy town it is sometimes thought to be. On the contrary, it is a lively and a friendly place with a first-class repertory theatre of long standing. Field archaeology is combined with an intelligently run museum. Municipal gardens and parks are plentiful, well designed and well tended. Flowers grow easily at Worthing.

Broadwater was the core of the young, lustily growing Worthing, and Broadwater Church is still the mother church of the town. But the place which now gives the strongest impression of an ancient heart is West Tarring, so named to distinguish it from Tarring Neville in the Ouse Valley.

Worthing has entirely surrounded but not swamped West Tarring, which obstinately refuses to be anything but a village. One long and narrow street called the High Street is lined with cottages mostly built in the seventeenth century. Their walls are of knapped flint, rough flint, pebble flint, white plaster and little red bricks, and the street is indented with dainty courtyards. At one end is a terrace called Parsonage Row Cottages, now a single house. It was built in the fifteenth century, and massive timber-framed walls support a roof of massive Horsham slabs. This lovely building was rescued from demolition in 1927 by the Sussex Archaeological Trust, and it is now a museum arranged so that the rooms look lived in.

West Tarring was originally called Terringes, and King Athelstan gave the manor to 'the Church of Christ at Canterbury' in 941. An archbishop's palace was built there in the thirteenth century, and it is now the parish hall. Much of the original outer flint wall remains, but the inside is covered with Victoriana. You catch exasperatingly small glimpses of what lies beneath.

A church was also built in the thirteenth century, and the original nave and aisle survive. The fifteenth-century tower supports a shingled spire, which is a notable landmark.

Eastward, Sompting is all but swallowed up, but the

Parsonage Row Cottages, West Tarring, now a single building housing an imaginative museum. It was built in the fifteenth century, and is just one building, probably the oldest in a long street of cottages, most of which were built in the seventeenth century. Worthing has surrounded West Tarring, but has not destroyed it. The village conveys the impression that it was the original heart round which the modern resort has developed.

church with its famous Saxon tower is mercifully not obscured. There is in fact an excellent view of it from the A27 road. It is about a thousand years old, and is the only one in the country with the gabled pyramidal cap called a 'Rhenish helm' because so many churches in the Rhine Valley are equipped with such towers.

The most prominent landmark further east is the modern-gothic Lancing College chapel, dramatically sited on the hilltop. Then you cross the River Adur and come to Shoreham, which to most of us means New Shoreham, its predecessor Old Shoreham having lost its value as a port through the silting up of the river. The parish church of St Mary de Haura was probably completed by about 1130, but it was extended later that century and early in the next. Although much was then pulled down, it still contains some of the richest architecture in the county.

A strange, ancient building graces the High Street. It has a chequered front, part flint and part Caen stone. It was built in the twelfth century and altered later, and may have been a customs house. It is now in the care of the Sussex Archaeological Trust and is known as the Marlipins.

Old Shoreham has a sturdy, much-restored Norman church a mile north of New Shoreham, and the downs and the meadows of the Adur estuary are nearby.

John landed at Shoreham in 1199 to succeed Richard I as king. Charles II left Shoreham in 1651 as a refugee for France, having stayed the night at an inn in Brighton.

The port is a busy place with a definitely industrial air, but it has a popular quarter for yachts. Boat building has been carried on since the Middle Ages.

The five miles from here to Brighton form a very congested district, which takes in industrial Portslade with the stacks of the power station dwarfing everything else. It also includes Southwick, whose green seems to have dropped down from the countryside. Suddenly you emerge from the streets of workshops to the broad vistas of the Hove Lagoon,

Brighton's municipal gardens are not only admired by residents and visitors but also studied by expert horticulturists. Tulip display at the Royal Pavilion North Gate.

THE
Leather Boutique
43
THE OLDEST HOUSE IN BRIGHTON
rrymores
TIQUE FURNITURE
CHINA & GLASS
GHEST PRICES GIVEN
BRIGHTON
SQUARE
OPEN
Serving

sunken gardens and lawns, with the bold sweep of the squares and the terraces in the background. Brighton begins at the end of the lawns, but you cannot tell the difference.

If I were asked to name three things which sprang to mind at the mention of Brighton, I should say the flowers, the Lanes and the Royal Pavilion. For three more, I should give the Regency architecture, the shops and the sea. These six factors constitute what one might call the essential Brighton, but you cannot dismiss Brighton as easily as that. Brighton is a very complex place with a complex history, and its nickname, 'London by the sea', is not undeserved.

The gardens of Brighton are by no means taken for granted; every year they excite the admiration of residents and visitors alike. Horticulturists make special journeys from overseas to see the spring displays, and their numbers include experts from that leading horticulturist country, Holland. Their season begins in February, when crocuses suddenly splash the grass with pools of colour. But the show really gets going at tulip time, and from then on there is a constant blaze of colour in the municipal gardens until the chrysanthemums of late autumn, with a really special effort to grace the Brighton Festival of the Arts in May.

The beds are never rested. This makes horticultural purists throw up their hands in horror, but no disaster has ever occurred. The tulips ought to catch 'tulip fire', and the wallflowers ought to get stunted and stringy, but they do not. Brighton's gardeners just take care to see that the beds are very well dug, very well manured and sometimes re-soiled. Intense conferences are held on colour schemes, which are worked out as meticulously as the discerning woman works out the colour schemes of her house.

The Lanes are old Brighton, once the small fishing town of Brighthelmston, and innumerable tourists go away believing that they have seen the medieval heart of a flourishing

The Lanes, Brighton, provide an excellent idea of what a medieval town was like, but in fact they are less medieval than they look. Owing to the raids of the French there are very few medieval buildings in Brighton, and the Lanes are mostly seventeenth and eighteenth century. But they were rebuilt on the pattern of their predecessors.

modern resort and business centre. The facts are otherwise. French raiders thoroughly sacked Brighthelmston in 1514, and as a result the town has no medieval buildings except St Nicholas's Parish Church, which stood on a hill outside the town. It took the little town a long time to recover, but restoration followed the old pattern, and so has subsequent rebuilding. The houses that line the winding alleys today are mostly of the eighteenth century, some later, and probably only one earlier. This is in Black Lion Street and may have been built in the sixteenth century. But the Lanes, because they are a faithful copy, provide a first-rate picture of what a medieval town was like, with their liberal overhangs, low doorways, softly lit shop fronts and dim interiors.

The Brighton Lanes are now a centre for the antique dealers of many lands, and Queen Mary, an expert, was a frequent visitor and purchaser at the little shops. The amount of material in the windows is bewildering, but system and careful arrangement lie behind the apparent disorder, and the Lanes dealers know the value of their merchandise. You must be prepared to pay a fair price, and genuine antiques are not cheap.

St Nicholas's gave way to St Peter's as the parish church in 1873. St Peter's was built between 1824 and 1828, and its impressive white tower faces down the Valley Gardens to the Old Steine, where the Brighthelmston fishermen used to mend their nets.

Unkind things are often said about the architecture of the Royal Pavilion, but nobody would wish to alter it in the slightest degree. In 1786-7 Henry Holland designed a pavilion which was classical, pure of line and pleasing. In 1815 the Prince Regent had the whole thing redesigned by John Nash, who produced the Oriental fantasy we have today.

Whoever goes to Brighton and Hove will be affected by the Regency architecture, whether he realizes it or not, and even if he knows nothing about architecture whatever. The strong,

St Peter's Church, Brighton, the town's parish church and one of the best examples of early Gothic revival in England. The architect was Sir Charles Barry, who won the work in competition before he was 30. The church was built in 1824 to 1828. Barry also won, in 1836, the competition to design the new Houses of Parliament.

flowing lines cannot fail to impress deeply, even if subconsciously. It is the beauty of the curve that is most striking, and you see it not only in the well-known terraces and crescents but also in individual buildings and little streets whose names you have not heard of and do not remember, in small, intimate bowfronts, which in Spain would make artists gurgle with delight. The two most famous crescents are Royal Crescent, the earliest of the Brighton crescents (built 1798-1807), faced with black tiles and still unexcelled; and Sussex Square, opening to the magnificent sweep of Lewes Crescent. The span of this crescent, built in the 1820s, is 840 ft, 200 ft wider than the Royal Crescent at Bath. Hove's smaller Brunswick Terrace and Brunswick Square follow a similar pattern.

One should not forget that other Brighton, the little back streets, once squalid and unsavoury but now considerably perked up under new paint and the pride of home ownership. Nor should one overlook (as if one could!) the new buildings. Some, like little Brighton Square, are altogether delightful; others, like Churchill Square, are an intriguing mixture; and the tall, individual blocks, are as horrible as they are anywhere.

Indeed, the whole town is a tantalizing medley of the beautiful and the brash, the exquisite and the downright ugly. And they say that once you have lived in Brighton you always go back.

Brighton has taken over a number of villages but has not overwhelmed them all. They include Rottingdean, a former fishing and farming village, as you can still sense. There is a small green, a duck pond, clusters of flint houses, a Norman and Early English church and tracks leading straight on to the downs.

The Prince Regent's Brighton extravaganza, the Royal Pavilion. The architect was John Nash, and his Oriental creation, built from 1815 to 1822, followed a classical house by Henry Holland (1786-7). The prince married Mrs Fitzherbert in 1785, and they went to Brighton together each year, but Mrs Fitzherbert never slept at either of the pavilions. She always took a house nearby, and in 1804 had one built. This now has a new facade and is the Y.M.C.A. building. The Prince became King George IV in 1820, and did not visit Brighton after 1827.

The first of the famous Brighton crescents, Royal Crescent. It was built between 1798 and 1807.

Stanmer Park, bought by Brighton Corporation in 1947 from the Chichester Estates Company. The park is part of the Stanmer Estate which comprises about 4,598 acres. The corporation bought the estate for £225,000.

Falmer, on the Lewes Road, has a magnificent barn attached to Court Farm. Telscombe, an absolutely unspoilt village, lies in a deep valley at the end of a long and winding cul-de-sac off the road from Newhaven to Lewes. Patcham has become a large suburb, but the original flint village of former farm cottages still lines a lane from the London Road to the edge of the downs. Stanmer is the estate village of Stanmer Park, once the home of the Earls of Chichester, the Pelhams, doughty fighters of the French. Beyond the beeches and parkland of Stanmer are Sir Basil Spence's characteristic buildings of the University of Sussex.

Newhaven and Seaford are sometimes linked together in the mind like Rye and Winchelsea or Brighton and Hove. In fact, the two are very dissimilar and both tend deliberately to stress their differences. Seaford likes to emphasize its residential and tourist attractions, while Newhaven is more industrial, and not only because of its port.

The harbour is, however, the chief reason for the existence of the town, and it grows steadily more important. In 1926 the Southern Railway Company took it over from the Newhaven Harbour Company, and it is therefore now owned by British Rail. British Rail have considerably expanded the port's activities by increasing passenger traffic with France through the big drive-on, drive-off ferries which sail to Dieppe. The quays also handle extensive import and export cargoes, and there is a large coastal trade.

Yet had it not been for a caprice of nature there would have been no Newhaven. The River Ouse flows into Seaford Bay, with Seaford on the east, Newhaven on the west, and tall cliffs either side. Until the sixteenth century the river joined the sea at Seaford; the eastward push of beach and silt built up a bank which turned the river from its southerly course towards the east, and Seaford had become a harbour, a port and a member of the Cinque Ports Confederation as a 'limb' of Hastings. Westward lay a village called Meeching. In 1570 a great storm forced a tremendous volume of flood

Expansion of the seaside resorts has meant an insidious nibbling into the downs. This photograph was taken at the northern end of Brighton.

water down the river, which burst through the shingle bank, poured through Meeching, and found the sea towards the west of the bay. By the early seventeenth century it had settled down more or less to the course it follows today. Seaford lost its harbour, and Meeching became Newhaven.

The port began to grow up along the banks of the river, and its fortunes, like the tides, have ebbed and flowed. It was not long before the silt began to take over. A channel was dug in the reign of Charles II, but this was not enough, and in 1731 the river was deepened and the harbour systematically developed. This soon brought a great deal of maritime prosperity. In the eighteenth century the stately ships on the West Indies run sailed in and out; steamships began the crossing to Dieppe in 1825. The port appeared to be on the decline just after the last war, but today British Rail hold it in high regard because it is the nearest south-coast port to London.

The parish church which stands on Castle Hill contains a lot of Norman work, including the tower. Nearby, from the top of the headland, you can see the whole bay spread before you like a map.

Seaford was left with a basin and no sea it it. Presently, the sea tried to come back, but by then it was unwelcome because some of the land had been built on. The sea was necessary, of course, when seaside holidays became the fashion, but only provided it took no liberties. So very expensive works were built, washed away, rebuilt, and have to be maintained to keep the sea where Seaford wants it. Occasionally, however, in one of its really nasty moods, the sea will still toss a few tons of concrete up to the promenade.

Very little remains of the old Seaford beyond the prominent parish church, which, though rebuilt in parts, contains Norman work, and has a list of vicars which starts in 1247. What Seaford has today is a wonderful countryside on

Misty morning in Telscombe. This is one of Brighton's villages. It came to the town through a bequest of the late Mr Ambrose Gorham, of Telscombe House. There are strict stipulations that the village should remain undisturbed in its fold in the downs.

201 BCD

its very doorstep. From the eastern edge of the town there is a clear eight-mile cliff walk to Eastbourne. If you reach Cuckmere Haven at low tide it is possible to wade across the river; otherwise you make a 2½-mile detour up the river to Exceat bridge and down the other side.

Eastbourne is one of the latest of the Sussex resorts and did not start in the holiday business until well after the middle of the last century. Then the place was properly laid out at the instigation of the Duke of Devonshire. You might almost be in Paris if you turn your back to the sea. Wide, tree-lined boulevards criss-cross one another, and houses of classic proportions with no Victorian fuss stand back from wide pavements.

Old East Bourne is about a mile inland and is carefully preserved. Here is the parish church (St Mary's), a large building of flint and stone, part late Norman, part fourteenth century, and here also are the timber-framed *Lamb Inn,* the sixteenth-century Old Parsonage and the eighteenth-century Manor House, now the Towner Art Gallery.

The eastern end of Beachy Head rises sharply from the boundaries of the town, and from these lower slopes banked parallel gardens are built up along the front. It is one of the loveliest seafronts I know. But going inland, the entire eastern end of the downs is boxed in by buildings which stretch the whole five miles up to Polegate.

Bexhill, five miles over the levels from Pevensey, is a surprisingly agreeable place. The slightly stuffy reputation that clings to it is no more deserved than is Worthing's. Outstanding among the buildings is the De La Warr Pavilion, beautifully proportioned, with clean, functional lines and curves. Its lawns lead right down to the sea. It was built in 1933-6 and such a building at that time was revolutionary. It contains concert and conference halls, a tea lounge and a restaurant. Old Bexhill, a mile from the front, boasts the parish church of St Peter's, founded in Norman times. Bexhill

Where Seaford town ends, Seaford Head begins. It is very dangerous indeed to go beyond this jutting point if the tide is coming in. The land falls considerably here and the incoming tide flows swiftly up to the chalk. Anybody the other side will be cut off and there is no way up the cliff.

did not rise to resort status until after 1880, when its population was about 2,000.

Hastings, Rye and Winchelsea have much in common historically. All three were members of the Cinque Ports Confederation (called the Five Ports until the sixteenth century, when the 'cinque' was adopted); all three suffered in the tit-for-tat raids between the English and the French navies; and all three suffered terribly from Channel tempests of unparalleled ferocity. But their triumphs and their tribulations were not necessarily shared. The misfortunes of one sometimes led to the good fortune of another.

The original Five Ports were Hastings, Romney, Hythe, Dover and Sandwich. Rye and Winchelsea were first attached to Hastings, but later became head ports. At the height of its power, Hastings contributed twenty ships for naval service and only Dover ever contributed more than that.

Whenever Hastings crops up in conversation I do not think first of William. I think of the great tawny cliffs which form the background to the town. They are most prominent at the eastern end, where they tower over the fishing boats; but they are also very noticeable from the promenade, as they rise over the hotels and other seafront buildings. If you are not careful you find yourself investing them with a personality. Occasionally they disappear, but then they come back again, peering blandly at you over the rooftops.

Hastings is the most historic of all the Sussex coastal towns, and it is, of course, a highly significant spot in the history of the nation. Though the battle of 1066 was fought six miles away, William made Hastings his headquarters, and later his principal port. It was probably William who built the first castle high up on the top of the cliff now called West Hill. This was most likely a timber structure, and was replaced about 1070 by Robert Count of Eu with something more solid in the proper Norman tradition. It is now a picturesque and much photographed ruin, and shares the hilltop with the ruins of the collegiate church of St Mary, also of the late eleventh century. This church was replaced in 1828 by a new building at the foot of the cliff. Space for it had to be dug from the rock, and its origin is reflected in its name, St Mary-in-the-Castle.

The De La Warr Pavilion, Bexhill was built in the 'thirties when architecture like this was exceptional. It provides shelter no matter from which direction the wind blows.

RX 152

Hastings was a port long before William arrived, and its name was Haestinges, derived from Haesta or Haesten, chief of the tribe of the Haestingas, who may have been Jutes. The harbour they used was no doubt developed and expanded by William, but all trace of it has vanished. Where the ships of the Saxons and the Normans lay safely sheltered from the storms is now a matter of guesswork. We only know the storms won in the end.

Everybody who lives anywhere near the Sussex coast is all too familiar with the fury of the south-west gales which rage up the Channel, blasting in shop windows, ripping up trees and hurling boulders from the shore to the highest promenade. These are trifles compared with the storms which battered the coast towards the end of thirteenth century. In 1286 and 1287 gales of particular violence first badly damaged the harbour at Hastings and then choked it with silt. During the next century the French followed up the ravages of nature with devastating raids, and eventually Hastings, senior member of the Cinque Ports Confederation, became a mere fishing village and did not begin to recover until the second half of the eighteenth century – apart from a brief revival in 1588, when it supplied ships and men to fight the Spanish Armada.

Prosperity returned with the discovery that the seaside was good for the health, and in the nineteenth century Hastings, with the newly built St Leonards, quickly attained the status of a major resort. Today, as with Brighton and Hove, you cannot tell when you are out of one and in the other. But when you go to that part of Hastings called the Old Town, there will be no confusion in your mind as to where you are. Here are the narrow, winding streets, little alleyways and timber-framed buildings, and here, also, are fragments of the old town wall built in the late fourteenth century as a defence against the two prevailing perils, the sea and the French.

The fishing quarter of Hastings. Lacking a harbour, vessels have to be hauled up the beach. The cliff in the background is sandstone rock and it glows amber in the sun. It is the end of one of the Wealden ridges.

Two churches in the Old Town, St Clement's and All Saints, are a direct link with the depredations of the French. Both were destroyed in a very bad raid in 1377. St Clement's was rebuilt in 1390, which makes it the oldest church in Hastings, and All Saints was rebuilt in the fifteenth century.

The Old Town leads straight to the foreshore and the fishing quarter, which really is a fishing quarter and not a gimmick for tourists. This area is called the Stade, a Saxon word which means landing place. As there is still no harbour, the luggers are hauled up the shingle beach, which is dominated by a group of tall, tarred, box-like structures called net shops, said to be unique in this country but more common in Spain. They are not shops in the accepted sense, but stores designed so that nets could be hung up to dry, thereby saving space when there was not a lot of room on the beach.

Four miles of sandstone cliffs stretch from Hastings to Fairlight Cove. A path goes the whole way, and on clear days the coast of France is visible from it. Shortly before you reach Fairlight you cross the Fire Hills. This unusual name has nothing to do with battles or beacons. It originates from flowers: in the spring the hills are a blaze of gorse.

There are several roads to Winchelsea from Fairlight. The one that appeals most to the imagination is the sea wall road, with marsh meadows on one side and on the other, the old enemy, the sea, ready to take advantage of the slightest weakness and come flooding in.

Though in may ways the fortunes of Winchelsea have been bound up with those of Rye and Hastings, in one respect its history is entirely different. Whereas Rye grew up bit by bit according to personal and official needs and wishes, Winchelsea was deliberately planned from start to finish. It antedated the new towns of the twentieth century by over six hundred years, and the king himself, Edward I, took a close interest in its design and construction. Winchelsea was

Strand Gate, Winchelsea, built in the thirteenth century and one of the original gates of the town.

to be a bastion of the realm, a function which it had already fulfilled as a member of the Cinque Ports, for there had been an older Winchelsea.

The new town was necessary because the older Winchelsea had suffered disaster: the sea had battered it to bits, and today we cannot even be sure exactly where the old town stood, although we know it was at sea level. New Winchelsea was built on a hill overlooking an ample harbour, fed by the estuary of the River Brede, and the people of old Winchelsea moved up to their hilltop homes in 1292.

The streets were wide and crossed one another at right angles, so that the town comprised a series of symmetrical blocks, like a Roman city. The whole town was ringed by defences, part timber, part earth, but of stone at vital places. Despite these defences the French got in. They made seven major attacks in the fourteenth and fifteenth centuries, and some of the larger buildings which they destroyed were not rebuilt.

Yet Winchelsea flourished, and it was not the French who ended her prosperity. It was, once again, the sea, though not through its violence. It quietly withdrew – sand bars appeared; the silt built up; and by the end of the fifteenth century Winchelsea's life as a port was over. Unlike Rye, Winchelsea could find no alternative livelihoood. Neglect and decay took their toll and when John Evelyn, the diarist, visited the town in 1652 he found it "all in rubbish, and a few despicable hovels and cottages only standing".

That is not the picture today. No town could be tidier or better cared for. But there is something curiously elusive about Winchelsea; it is as hard to picture her former glory as it is easy to picture Rye's. The grid system of the roads remain, but there is no feeling of a town, yet still less the feel of a village. There is no quiet echo of battles lost and won, and the first-time visitor views with astonishment the stark battlements of the Strand Gate, and even more so the New Gate, now way out in the meadows and with no apparent connection whatever with Winchelsea.

Another surprise is the half-ruined or half-finished church of St Thomas (it is not certain which). It was probably begun early in the fourteenth century and it is clear that an

The parish church at Winchelsea. Is it half finished or half ruined?

impressive structure was planned for a whole block was allocated to it. The chancel and the side chapels are left, completed. What happened? The French have been blamed, but a number of factors might have been responsible, including, perhaps, the Black Death of 1349.

John Wesley preached his last open-air sermon on October 6, 1790, at Winchelsea under an ash tree near the church. There is an ash tree there now, not the one the preacher stood under, but a scion of it. Wesley often preached under the ash tree, and like Evelyn, he was shocked at the surrounding desolation, which he described as "that poor skeleton of Ancient Winchelsea".

Near the Strand Gate a narrow platform has been cut into the steep earth cliff. This is the look-out, and from this position a watch was kept for French ships. Today you are directed to it for the view, as extensive as ever but over level pasture instead of sea. Just over two miles across what was once a wide inlet from the Channel, the houses of Rye cluster round a church on top of a hill.

Rye on a warm September day is sheer bliss. The streets are quiet and uncrowded and you can stroll in comfort, your eyes on the ancient buildings, which are seen to their best advantage in the mellow light, and then on the marsh pasture below, which stretches far away into a golden haze.

Rye has been famous for centuries but some parts are more famous than others. This is due more to the visitor's whim than to any authentic superiority. Mermaid Street, world famous, is wholly delightful but so also is Watchbell Street and any number of little streets leading away from Church Square at the top of the town, where the parish church rises high above the houses, a conspicuous landmark for miles over the marsh.

The thing to do in Rye is just walk and never mind the cobbles, and when you come to the *Mermaid Inn,* as every visitor is bound to do, don't be content with the picturesque view from the street. The massive timber work is best seen

These level pastures between Winchelsea and Rye were once the wide estuary of the River Brede. The photograph was taken from the look-out, Winchelsea.

from the courtyard, which you reach through an arch or from the interior. The *Mermaid* is the largest of Rye's medieval houses.

Whichever direction you take from Church Square it will be downhill, and if you go south, east or west you come to a sharp drop, almost a cliff edge. From any point on this eminence the level land of the marsh is spread out before you for a very long way. If, now, you half close your eyes you will find it easy to picture the waves curling where the flat pastures lie, and ships sailing where the sheep and the cattle graze; and that is how it was. Rye is a port which the sea has deserted.

Its history reaches back to the days of the Saxons, from whom its name is derived. The Oxford Dictionary of English Place Names heroically traces it back to mean 'an island' or 'at the island', *atter ie,* then *atterie.* Finally all was dropped but 'Rie'. Rye had grown to a port of considerable consequence by the middle of the twelfth century. Rye and Winchelsea became Cinque Ports as 'members' of Hastings in 1191, and when Hastings declined, the two towns, as befitted their rising status, were made head ports with the same privileges and responsibilities as the original five.

Rye was at the peak of its commercial and naval importance in the thirteenth and fourteenth centuries. It contributed five ships to the Cinque Ports fleet, handled overseas and coastal shipping, was the home of a flourishing fishing fleet, and maintained an important market and an equally important pottery.

Friction with France was normal, and battles, official and unofficial, were joined with gusto. Towns were burnt both sides of the Channel. One day in 1377 the French burnt Rye to the ground. This created not only great hardship and suffering at the time but also acute impoverishment in the future, and led to a measure which has been the cause of a

Mermaid Street, Rye. The building on the right is the Mermaid Inn, still containing medieval work. The cellar under the hall is probably thirteenth century, but apart from that the earliest work is fifteenth century. This street was the entry to the town for the traveller from overseas. Most of it dates from the fifteenth to the seventeenth century.

Ypres Tower, Rye. It has no connection with Ypres in Flanders. It was bought in 1430 by John de Ypres when the town was short of money owing to the depredations of the French. There was a stipulation that the tower could be occupied in time of war. In 1518 the town got it back. It was built about 1270 and until John de Ypres bought it, the name was Baddings Tower.

Watchbell Street, Rye. It is lined with homely houses like these and connects Church Square at the top of the town with the Strand, the medieval trading area, though no buildings of this era remain.

misunderstanding ever since. To raise money, a part of the defences called Baddings Tower, built about 1250, was sold in 1430 to a private buyer. His name was John de Ypres, and the structure became known as the Ypres Tower, the 'castle' of Rye. It had nothing to do with that other, even better known Ypres in Flanders.

Rye remained one of the best harbours on the south coast until the latter half of the sixteenth century. Then the silting up began. Steadily the sea went back. Now it is two miles off, and modern Rye Harbour is a small, untidy place where the Rother thrusts through the shingle to the sea.

I do not share the view sometimes expressed that Rye is a mere museum piece. It has brought into the twentieth century the advantages of past centuries but not their disadvantages, a state of affairs much appreciated by Henry James, the novelist, who lived in Rye from 1897 until he died in 1916. It has retained a grace and harmony, but it has shed the smells, diseases and squalor.

There are, however, more positive and active aspects of life in Rye. The fishing fleet is not what it was but the fishing boats still go out down the Rother; ships are still built; and Rye pottery is known far beyond these shores. Rye is also a business, shopping and agricultural centre, with two market days a week, Wednesday and Thursday. It is one of the main centres of the Marsh, which covers 56,000 acres and carries 200,000 sheep and 5,000 cattle. It is also a focal point for a big area of the Weald. Rye has achieved the right balance between a thriving local life and tourism: visitors are welcome and throng the streets in summer, but they have not taken over.

I have often looked westward from Rye and tried to imagine all of Sussex, its hills and valleys and those Wealden ridges, its forests and rivers, its obstinate fields of clay and the long white wall of the cliffs. It is so lovely and so vulnerable, and there are many predators – it could so easily be lost. The price of beauty, like the price of freedom, is eternal vigilance.

INDEX

Page numbers in bold type refer to pages of illustrations